THE DUTY TO STAND ASIDE

Aerial photo of Hamburg bombing, July 1943.
Photo: Imperial War Museum

THE DUTY TO STAND ASIDE

Nineteen Eighty-Four
and the Wartime Quarrel of
George Orwell and Alex Comfort

by Eric Laursen

AK PRESS

The Duty to Stand Aside, by Eric Laursen
© 2018 Eric Laursen

This edition © 2018 AK Press (Chico, Edinburgh)

ISBN: 978-1-84935-318-2
E-ISBN: 978-1-84935-317-5
Library of Congress Control Number: 2017957068

AK Press   AK Press
370 Ryan Ave. #100   33 Tower St.
Chico, CA 95973   Edinburgh EH6 7BN
USA   Scotland
www.akpress.org   www.akuk.com
akpress@akpress.org   ak@akedin.demon.co.uk

The above addresses would be delighted to provide you with the
latest AK Press distribution catalog, which features books, pamphlets, zines, and stylish apparel published and/or distributed
by AK Press. Alternatively, visit our websites for the complete
catalog, latest news, and secure ordering.

Cover design by John Yates, www.stealworks.com
Printed in the USA on recycled paper

This book is dedicated to Mary V. Dearborn.

Table of Contents

PREFACE

Not long after the last guns were fired, World War II became known as the Good War—though we don't know who coined the phrase. It was always a strange way to refer to the worst slaughter in human history, but it quickly became commonplace—so much so that it has been used in the titles of book, films, in TV commercials, and a blizzard of articles, papers, and memoirs. By 1984, when Studs Terkel published his oral history of the period—largely from the American point of view—he had to add a touch of irony by putting his title in quotation marks: *The "Good War."*

The phrase stuck for many reasons, the most obvious being the hugely repellent nature of the regimes on one side of the conflict. World War II was a righteous war—a "Crusade in Europe," according to the title of Allied Supreme Commander Dwight D. Eisenhower's wartime memoir—because it ended the threat of world domination by Nazism, fascism, and Japanese militarism. Certainly, this was a good thing—the liberation of the Nazi death camps and the revelation of the vast crimes of Hitler's regime exposed mass murder and outright genocide on a scale that had never been practiced before. It is frightening to consider what the world would be like today if the Axis had won or even had fought the war to a stalemate.

But does that make World War II a good war?

Many of the leaders of the Allied war effort had supported or sympathized with one or another of the totalitarian regimes at various times before the German invasion of Poland. Some had quietly aided them or, as in Spain, actively undermined their opponents. Then there was the war itself: it changed the world by rewriting the maps of Europe and Asia, by introducing new technologies of death that have exposed enormous human populations to mass destruction, and by vastly expanding the political and economic elite's expertise at surveillance, thought control, and police repression.

Some of the war's most terrible and enduring innovations, like "area bombing" of civilian populations, were devised not by Berlin but by democratic Britain. Napalm was developed at Harvard University and first deployed by the U.S. Army Air Force on Berlin in March 1944. The atomic bomb, under development by Germany in the early days of the war, was brought into being and inflicted on a civilian Japanese population by an American government already looking to cement its dominance in the coming postwar order. Other major powers got their hands on the technology as quickly as they could. Ever since, life on Earth has depended on the judgment and sanity of a small collection of politicians, dictators, and warlords, many of whom would more appropriately be standing trial for assorted crimes against humanity than occupying positions of power.

"War is the health of the State," the American radical journalist Randolph Bourne wrote in the last months of World War I. Since World War II, war is more accurately the addiction of the State, as one or more nuclear powers have been pursuing some "conflict" (the word "war" appears less and less as an official designation) in some part of the world almost continuously. Above all, World War II produced an immeasurable expansion of the scope, pervasiveness, and ambition of the State itself.

On neither side of the conflict did governments stumble into this; from the start, all were focused on how the war would enable them to shape the world that followed it. Plenty of people outside centers of power analyzed the trend correctly at the time, but they were either dismissed as pacifists or defeatists or else kept their opinions to themselves. Nevertheless, they created a legacy that has complicated the task of making war in the decades since the Bomb was dropped and in a few cases has helped to stop or end wars.

This book is about two remarkable English writers, both of whom grasped the larger implications of their government's actions in World War II but took opposite sides in the debate over how critics of the State should respond. George Orwell was a more or less libertarian socialist who first opposed and then wholeheartedly joined the war effort. Alex Comfort was an anarchist and pacifist who distrusted his government's intentions and worked to expose the warfare on civilians that it initiated as part of the struggle to defeat Hitler.

Orwell went on to author two of the most widely read fictional works in the English language, *Animal Farm* and *Nineteen Eighty-Four*. Today he is widely see as a kind of secular saint on account of his keen analysis of the misuse of language in politics and his unbending opposition to totalitarianism on both the left and the right. In the process, the inconsistencies, excesses, and tortuousness of some of his political writings have been glossed over or ignored. In his zeal to defeat fascism and, later, Stalinism, Orwell kept his misgivings about his own government largely to himself, rationalized some of them away, and lost no opportunity to tag its critics—including a young poet, physician, and biologist named Alex Comfort—as "objectively" pro-German or pro-totalitarian.

Comfort is remembered today mainly as the author of an extremely successful 1972 book, *The Joy of Sex*. But in the 1940s he was rapidly building a reputation as both a talented writer and a radical critic of war and the State. An influential treatise he published in 1950, *Authority and Delinquency in the Modern State: A Criminological Approach to the Problem of Power*, attempts to answer the questions he had begun asking during the war: What sort of people order atrocities? Why do they so often find their way into positions of leadership? And how does the State create the conditions for them to flourish and to act? Like *Nineteen Eighty-Four*, the analysis in *Authority and Delinquency* grew partly out of Comfort and Orwell's public quarrel during the war and the friendlier dialogue between them once it was over.

Comfort once described Orwell as "a man unsparing of himself, facing excruciating moral decisions (as we all were) in the dark." My goal in this book is to bring their dialogue back into the light, to understand how their decisions apply in the world the war created, and perhaps to offer a way for opponents of war to think about the false choices the State places before us when it wants our approval to unleash another spasm of violence. But the heart of this story is the relationship between two passionately committed defenders of freedom, the unexpected twists and turns it took in the years after the war, and its strange and long-hidden end in the months before Orwell's death.

* * *

This book touches on four matters of history: the origins of area bombing as a military doctrine, the air war between Britain and Germany during World War II, pacifist and antibombing campaigns and the anarchist movement in Britain, and the political response of British writers, artists, and intellectuals to the war. A great deal of excellent scholarship covers each of these areas, which I have made use of, along with many primary sources, in setting the stage for this story.

As for the protagonists, almost everything George Orwell ever wrote, down to the last jotting, has now been published thanks to Peter Davison, editor of *The Complete Works* and *The Lost Orwell*. Alex Comfort's wartime and postwar publications and broadcasts are mostly out of print but obtainable; his papers relating to this period are in the archives of University College London. Much of what appears in this book I found in the Comfort papers, which were invaluable in making sense of the developing relationship between Comfort and Orwell.

I am especially indebted to Nicholas Comfort for his memories of his father, not to mention his encouragement and help with sources. Arthur Salmon generously shared his correspondence with Nicholas Moore and his memories of interviews with Alex Comfort. His excellent critical study, *Alex Comfort* (Boston: Twyane Publishers, 1978), was also very helpful, as was Nicholson Baker's wonderful *Human Smoke: The Beginnings of World War II, the End of Civilization* (New York: Simon & Schuster, 2008). I am very grateful to several wise persons who read and critiqued my manuscript at various stages, principally David Goodway and Kristian Williams, who brought their vast knowledge of British anarchism, British literature, and Orwell to bear, and also to Larry Gara. Richard Overy of the University of Exeter generously read and commented on the manuscript, corrected errors, and sent me in the right direction on several important issues.

The Plainfield Biographers' Group, including Lina Bernstein, Mary V. Dearborn, David Perkins, Heather Clark, and Robert and Mary Bagg, was not only supportive but provided invaluable—which is to say, unsparing—criticism each step of the way. The Autonolistas of New York

City—Christopher Cardinale and Melissa Jameson—were as supportive and helpful as ever, as was David Wyner. Straw Dog Writers Guild provided my first opportunity to present some of this material in public at its monthly Writers Read event in Ashfield, Massachusetts. Jeremy Rehwaldt copyedited my manuscript, corrected my grammar, and cut out excess verbiage. And I am once again very grateful to AK Press for its great support and commitment; I encourage everyone who reads this book to support AK.

I. THE MORAL LENS

The summer of 1943 found George Orwell, English socialist man of letters, reaching the end of his patience with his
job at the BBC. The cultural programs and commentary he
had been producing for the Indian and East Asian outposts
of the British Empire were designed to counter German
wartime radio transmissions. These broadcasts were not
quite propaganda: he was allowed "reasonable freedom of
speech" despite being (in his words) "an independent and
more or less 'agin the government' commentator," and he
could contribute to outside publications as well. But the
job was boring. After two years at the network, Orwell,
who had just turned forty, longed to go back to his own
writing and journalism.

Privately, too, he complained about the cumbersome
process of getting his scripts cleared and occasionally being
compelled to say things on air that he had a strong feeling
were not true. "I am regularly alleging in all my newsletters
that the Japanese are plotting to attack Russia," he confided in his diary, "although I don't believe this to be so."[1]

One of the poets whose work Orwell featured occasionally on his cultural programs was Alex Comfort, a
talented twenty-two-year-old who was taking medical

training at the Royal London Hospital and beginning independent research in biochemistry. Neither Orwell nor Comfort was spending World War II in the military. Orwell, who had been badly wounded while fighting in the Spanish Civil War and was showing signs of the tuberculosis that would ultimately kill him, was declared unfit for military service. Wishing passionately to contribute to this new war against fascism, he had applied repeatedly to enlist but had to settle for a volunteer slot in Britain's civil defense force, the ragtag, ill-equipped Home Guard.

There was never any question of Comfort serving in any capacity except as a medic or firewatcher during air raids: he was missing three and a half fingers of his left hand, the result of a botched attempt to make gunpowder for fireworks at age fourteen. But he would not have

George Orwell, 1946.
Photo: Vernon Richards, Archivio Berneri

enlisted even if he could. Comfort was a dedicated, outspoken pacifist and—by the end of the war—an anarchist who charged at every possible opportunity that Britain's wartime leaders were ordering atrocities as bad as some of Hitler's and that intellectuals who did not denounce their own government had "sacrificed their responsible attitude to humanity."[2] He made it his business in particular to expose as war crimes the British and American air raids against German and occupied cities—a campaign the Allies' political leaders regarded as the key to victory and that was popular with much of the public to boot.

Not surprisingly, given their vastly different attitudes about the conflict, the two men attacked each other repeatedly in print. Orwell initiated the exchange with a review of Comfort's first novel. Their dialogue continued principally in the American magazine *Partisan Review* and the British social democratic newspaper *Tribune*— the latter in the form of an exchange of verse during the summer of 1943 that became a minor classic of English polemic poetry—and in private conversation and correspondence. But their relationship was more complicated than this suggests. Over this same period, they developed a cautious friendship based on Orwell's admiration for Comfort's poetry—though not his fiction—and Comfort's respect for Orwell's incisive political commentary as well as his conduct as a Loyalist volunteer in the Spanish Civil War.

Their friendship grew into an active collaboration when the government began prosecuting anarchists and antiwar activists toward the end of the war. It cooled when the Cold War again highlighted their ideological differences, but it endured, at least so far as Comfort knew, until just before Orwell's death in 1950.

By then, *Animal Farm* and *Nineteen Eighty-Four* had been published, and Orwell was on his way to becoming one of the most admired writers and moral voices of the postwar era—to readers from an astonishingly wide range of political perspectives. Comfort would become a well-known and controversial figure in Britain in 1961, when he and thirty-one other antinuclear activists were sentenced to a month in prison for organizing a mass

Alex Comfort, 1943.
Photo: Vernon Richards, Archivio Berneri

sit-down demonstration in Trafalgar Square. In 1972 he would achieve worldwide best-sellerdom when his illustrated manual for couples, *The Joy of Sex*, was published. Comfort, who died a half century after Orwell, deeply admired his onetime adversary and, although they only met in person once, regarded him as a friend.

Writing thirty years after Orwell's passing, Comfort regretted the tone they had taken in their wartime quarrel. "We had publicly misrepresented one another," he wrote. "I probably mistook him for a hard-line Marxist, while he mistook me for another of [John] Middleton Murry's equivocal disciples,"[3] alluding to the poet and critic who had notoriously written that Hitler was "doing the dirty work of the Lord" and whose literary journal, the *Adelphi*, had helped launch the writing careers of both Orwell and Comfort.[4]

While they disagreed sharply about the morality of war, about collaboration with the State, and later about the choices the Cold War posed for artists and writers outside the Soviet bloc, Comfort believed he and Orwell were essentially on the same side: against authoritarianism and in favor of a society that relied on cooperation and community rather than capitalism and an overweening State.

For the most part, he was right. But in the 1990s it became known that in the last years of his life, as the Cold War was settling in, Orwell drew up a list of notable individuals he believed had pro-Soviet or insufficiently anti-Soviet tendencies. He entrusted the list to an employee in a propaganda branch of the Foreign Office. Included were writers and economists, political activists and broadcasters, and celebrities such as Charlie Chaplin and Michael Redgrave.

One of the names was that of Alex Comfort. "Is pacifist-anarchist," Orwell noted. "Main emphasis anti-British. Subjectively pro-German during war, appears temperamentally pro-totalitarian. Not morally courageous. Has a crippled hand. Very talented."[5]

The picture of Comfort thus presented was objectively a great distortion. Comfort was not "anti-British," just deeply critical of the British government. He was not "pro-German" in any sense, and, as an anarchist, he was the furthest thing from "pro-totalitarian." Nothing that has emerged from the Foreign Office papers in succeeding decades, however, suggests that Comfort or anyone else on Orwell's list saw their career suffer as a result of the list or that anyone in any other part of the government ever saw it. Some of the names were published in 1998, but the full document, including Comfort's name, was only released by the Foreign Office in 2002, two years after Comfort's death. Comfort suffered a massive stroke in 1991 and spent the rest of his life under nursing care; his son believes he never knew that Orwell had named him.[6]

When the list became known, it created a sensation among both Orwell admirers and detractors. How could the author of *Nineteen Eighty-Four*, who in fact had finished his dystopian novel less than six months before making the list, have done something so redolent of Stalinist ideological denunciation? Did Orwell himself have an authoritarian streak? Had his hatred of the Soviet tyranny gotten the better of his personal judgment? Was his final illness or an old romantic attachment a factor?

Some people on the list were personal enemies; one individual, with whom Orwell had worked at the BBC, may have lobbied to keep *Animal Farm* from being published. Other than responding to Orwell's attacks in the press, however, Comfort had done him no harm, and there is plenty of evidence besides that Orwell regarded Comfort with respect. They discussed *Nineteen Eighty-Four* when the novel was still in its early stages, and some of Comfort's writings in the last years of the war and the first years following may have influenced its development or at least reflected similar concerns. Their exchanges may also have informed *Authority and Delinquency in the Modern*

State, Comfort's 1950 treatise on the pathology of State power that serves as a partial bookend to Orwell's novel.

Can we make sense of the complicated feelings between these two remarkable writers and the way their relationship ended? Their similarities are just as important as their differences. Comfort and Orwell shared a deep conviction that political engagement, especially for writers and artists, was a moral responsibility, and both tended to assess political issues first and foremost through a moral lens. That is why they attacked each other so strongly and at times unfairly during the war; it is also why, once they discovered they had common concerns, they became friends. Orwell would not have included Comfort on his Foreign Office list if he hadn't cared what Comfort thought, wrote, and advocated.

Neither was concerned only with the war against Germany and the proper way to respond to it. They were both anxious about the world the war would create: dominated by an ever more powerful state apparatus, ever more threatening weapons, and, they feared, a power elite increasingly adept at turning the masses into apathetic observers rather than engaged political participants. How to respond? Orwell feared that anarchism and pacifism were dead ends leading only to defeatism, detachment, and perhaps not-so-passive acceptance; Comfort believed that collaboration with the State must end in acceptance of its methods and acquiescence to the "criminals" in charge.

These were not theoretical issues for either Orwell or Comfort; they reflected events taking place literally in the writers' own backyard: the London of the war years. And they have lost none of their urgency since, as warfare and mass killing have assumed a far more mechanized and impersonal character and as wars themselves are euphemized as police actions, counterinsurgencies, and nation-building exercises. Each time a purportedly "good war" is launched—the U.S.-led invasions of Afghanistan and Iraq, the international intervention in Libya to oust Muammar el-Qaddafi from power, Saudi Arabia's U.S.-backed war against Islamist Yemeni rebels—the conflict assumes a more complex and problematic form, and the questions that Comfort and Orwell raised must be asked again.

II. A CLASH OF TEMPERAMENTS

Aside from radio listeners who occasionally heard Orwell's broadcasts, the audiences that knew George Orwell and Alex Comfort during the war years were largely the British and, to a limited extent, American intelligentsia, mostly on the left. Their initial quarrel—to stand aside or to join the ranks—was quite stark.

"Pacifism is objectively pro-Fascist," Orwell declared. Its proponents "write mentally dishonest propaganda and degrade literary criticism to mutual arse-licking." Whatever their philosophical reasoning, pacifists could reasonably be lumped in with British profascists and America Firsters as silly, dangerous, and disloyal.[1]

Comfort, on the other hand, argued that holding to an antiwar position and maintaining independence from the State was an entirely appropriate response. He attacked writers and artists who turned propagandist in support of the war, and called on artists and intellectuals to expose their own government's atrocities and outrages, even if they believed victory by the other side would be a calamity. To support the war was to ignore the hypocrisy of Britain's political leaders, many of whom, just a few years earlier, had been all too willing to tolerate the rise of fascism—or worse.

Comfort was taking up again an argument that had raged all through World War I, as some intellectuals adopted their country's side in the conflict and others chose to stand apart—on principle, on political grounds, in solidarity with the millions who would die uselessly, or on the basis of some combination of the three. In the United States, when the progressive philosopher and social thinker John Dewey declared his support for the war, arguing that it could be a means of spreading democracy, his former student, the radical journalist Randolph Bourne, felt betrayed. "What concerns us here," he wrote in "War and the Intellectuals," an article for the literary magazine the *Seven Arts*, "is the relative ease with which the pragmatic intellectuals, with Professor Dewey at the head, have moved out their philosophy, bag and baggage, from education to war."

> The war sentiment, begun so gradually but so perseveringly by the preparedness advocates who came from the ranks of big business, caught hold of one after another of the intellectual groups. . . . The intellectuals, in other words, have identified themselves with the least democratic forces in American life. They have assumed the leadership for war of those very classes whom the American democracy has been immemorially fighting. Only in a world where irony was dead could an intellectual class enter war at the head of such illiberal cohorts in the avowed cause of world liberalism and world democracy.[2]

Bourne—and later Comfort—argued not only that the war was wrong but that artists and intellectuals had a particular responsibility to resist it. Orwell responded that, in any conflict of the magnitude of World War II, there was no responsible way to avoid taking sides. On top of this, Orwell held a deep distrust of the intelligentsia on the left, the product of his experience during the Spanish Civil War, which led him to suspect that much of the Left was only too ready to reflexively support totalitarian government in the form of Stalinism once they heard the call from Moscow. Comfort did not share this fear.

Orwell's antifascism led him to offer his services to politicians he had distrusted and even reviled before the war. To him, the imperative to defeat Hitler was just too powerful, and anarchists and pacifists "who are convinced of the wickedness both of armies and of police forces" practiced a moral absolutism that actually made them "much more intolerant and inquisitorial than the normal person."[3]

Perhaps the chance to work within the system was a bit of a relief to Orwell, given his prickly relationship with the Left. Comfort denounced his government, urged his readers to resist the war effort, and warned that "Hitler's greatest and irretrievable victory . . . was when he persuaded the English people that the only way to lick Fascism was to imitate it."[4]

But temperament may have played a role in his case as well: in contrast to Orwell, Comfort was too deeply critical of the system to entertain working within it for any political goal.

Yet, while he resolutely denounced pacifists in public and criticized anarchism as a political philosophy, Orwell's own brand of socialism—never precisely defined—veered toward the antibureaucratic and libertarian, and he shared many of the anarchists' suspicions about the people directing the war on Britain's behalf, their motives, and his own assigned role in the war effort. Biographer Bernard Crick, a political scientist, concluded that Orwell "did not accept anarchism in principle, but had, as a socialist who distrusted state power, a speculative and personal sympathy with anarchists."[5]

Comfort, who could see no good intentions behind his government's conduct, was not really, as Orwell imagined, a pacifist of the "turn-the-other-cheek" variety or a defeatist who simply believed that Britain should withdraw from the war because it was doomed to lose. He was ready to endorse armed resistance to the Germans, so long as that resistance was indigenous and not led by people who aspired merely to replace one murderous regime with another that might be nearly as bad—not so different from the stance Orwell himself had assumed during the Spanish Civil War.

Both Comfort and Orwell kept their distance from high political theory. When it came to any matter that deeply disturbed them—Soviet apologists, in Orwell's case, or rationalizers of total war, in Comfort's—both were capable of sternly categorical, borderline-unreasonable pronouncements. "[Orwell's] political doctrines were really moral doctrines in disguise,"[6] concluded George Woodcock, the Canadian writer and anarchist who was a friend of both men, and Cyril Connolly once quipped that his friend Orwell "could not blow his nose without moralising on conditions in the handkerchief industry."[7] Repeatedly during the 1940s, Comfort referred to the warlords and masters of the State not only as war criminals but also as "filth" and "criminal psychopaths."

Partisan Review, the American quarterly then making its pilgrimage from communism to Trotskyism to anticommunism and to which both Orwell and Comfort contributed, had a similar moralistic inclination, and both writers maintained a close correspondence with one of its most prominent editors, the anarchist Dwight Macdonald. Both were concerned not just with totalitarianism in the fascist and communist states but also with how something of the sort could develop in the democracies—fears that Orwell would take to a logical conclusion in *Nineteen Eighty-Four*.[8]

Both hoped, guardedly, that the war itself would spark a positive social transformation. Orwell anticipated a peaceful socialist revolution, which he expected to grow out of the collective nature of the war effort itself.[9] Comfort, in his more positive moments, hoped for a widespread refusal to serve that would lead to the end of war, capitalism, and the State. Orwell actually shared many of Comfort's concerns about the conduct of intellectuals who joined the propaganda effort during wartime—despite which he was willing, at first, to risk contamination to do his bit at the BBC.

In their intellectual approach, the two writers—Orwell, an indifferent pupil who had not attended university and worked his way up from obscurity through leftist journalism, and Comfort, a Cambridge-educated wunderkind—were very different. Comfort was still in his early twenties during the war; he had come of age politically when still quite young and was confident in his basic principles. Orwell was nearly twenty years older and had only become politically engaged well into adulthood.

Applying an academic cliché despite its oversimplification, Comfort was the fox who knows many things, Orwell the hedgehog who knows one big thing. Orwell's writings resemble a vast, ongoing testament, with earlier entries constantly being revisited and revised as the author encountered new information and new perspectives. Only his two major novels, plus *Down and Out in Paris and London*, *Homage to Catalonia*, and some of the essays feel complete and unimprovable. Comfort, conditioned by his practice as a research scientist, tended to treat problems as puzzles. He would examine and analyze each one until he had the answer, which he would then write up definitively and move on—a process he followed through an astonishing succession of fields, from biology and gerontology to anarchist theory to sexual practice and culture and then, late in life, to physics and human consciousness.

Comfort and Orwell were quite different physically as well. Orwell was a lanky, gaunt, gloomy man, "with worn Gothic features accentuated by the deep vertical furrows that ran down the cheeks and across the corners of the mouth," as Woodcock later described him.* Although reserved—even chilly—and very austere and serious in private life, he was not a loner, enjoyed the company of women, and maintained warm friendships with both liberal and conservative writers, which made him a success at pulling together cultural programming at the BBC, however much the job bored him.

Comfort—boyish, slight, and with a roundish, bespectacled face—was gaining a reputation as a leading member of the New Romantics, a group of young poets who made a stir in British literary circles in the 1940s. Nicholas Moore, John Bayliss, George Barker, and Henry Treece are some of the other names that were well-known at the time, with Dylan Thomas sometimes attached. The group was attempting to revive what Comfort later described as a rhetorical tradition in English poetry that they traced from Dryden and Pope through the Romantics, principally Byron and Shelley, a tradition that lent itself to grand statements about moral issues but, they felt, had been left behind in the austerely modernist poetry of W. H. Auden and his circle. Comfort and his allies sought to harness this tradition to express, among other things, their opposition to what they regarded as the "insanity"—Comfort's word—of a political system that instigated the mass slaughter of the war.[10]

Orwell had a good deal of sympathy for their efforts and a fair understanding of what motivated them. Poets such as Treece and Comfort, he said in a 1943 broadcast, "have it as the background of their thoughts that the basis for a decent society is already there, and on the other hand that the very existence of civilization is menaced." In 1900, Orwell reflected, most people—"and that would include most of the poets"—would not have believed that, just a few years later, one would be able to fly easily from

---

* "Rather like a tired bloodhound (though less majestic), which is perhaps what he was," Nicholas Moore, who met Orwell in the 1940s, commented in a November 6, 1980 letter to Comfort scholar Arthur Salmon.

London to Calcutta while the Jews would face greater persecution than any they had suffered since the Middle Ages.
Yet "anyone born within this century takes both facts for
granted." The younger poets thus "find themselves in a
world which has all the potentialities of peace and plenty
combined with the *fact* of destruction and hatred."[11]

Comfort edited a little magazine called *Poetry Folios*,
anthologies, and annuals devoted to the New Romantics
that caught Orwell's attention ("I believe there could be
a public for that kind of thing nowadays," he said in a
letter to Comfort).[12] But his medical and scientific work
kept him constantly busy—he studied the shell pigments
of mollusks and would soon be doing important work on
the aging process in animals and humans—which meant
that most of his literary friendships and collaborations
were by correspondence. He was nothing like the sex guru
many people assumed him to be from his later writings and
was living quite domestically with his first wife. In person, Comfort was warm and witty, a font of nonstop talk,
knowledge, and opinions.

Because they were British, perceptions of class complicated Orwell and Comfort's relationship. Orwell was a
product of "the lower-upper-middle class"—that is, as he
used to say, "the upper-middle class that is short of money."[13]

His father had been a civil servant in British India and
his mother's father was a French merchant in Burma, but,
as a socialist, he liked to adopt a quasi-proletarian pose.
In *The Road to Wigan Pier*, he famously skewered British
eccentrics and utopians of the Left, worrying they would
make it culturally impossible for ordinary people to accept
socialism. In particular, he scorned what he referred to as
"nancy poets" from Oxford and Cambridge and "parlour
Bolsheviks such as Auden & [Stephen] Spender"—the
poets from whom Comfort and the New Romantics were
trying to differentiate themselves.[14] Comfort was a grad-
uate of Trinity College, Cambridge, as were some of the

other New Romantics, which may be one reason Orwell accused them of "money-sheltered ignorance" in protesting their government's conduct of the war.[15]

In Comfort's case, Orwell was wrong about both the money and the sheltering. As a medical trainee in London, Comfort was treating victims of the German air raids that were still hitting the city, although less frequently, in the months after the Blitz. As for his position in the British caste system, it was almost exactly the opposite of what Orwell imagined. Comfort was an only child whose father worked in London local government and whose mother was a former schoolteacher; both came from lower middle-class families and were only able to send him to Highgate School, then to Cambridge and his medical training, with the help of scholarships and a good deal of scrimping and saving. Orwell, by contrast, came from a genteel background and had attended Eton College, the crown jewel of the English public-school network, before joining the Imperial Indian Police.

Their views on war aside, Orwell and Comfort had some points in common. One was an unfortunate fascination with explosives. Comfort's amateur experiment with fireworks had cost him several fingers. Orwell loved to tinker at bomb-making as well; once, in the Home Guard, he loaded the wrong type of projectile into a mortar, resulting in one batterymate losing his front teeth and another being knocked unconscious for twenty-four hours.[16]

But Orwell also shared with Comfort a deep concern about the way the politics of fascism, appeasement, and militarism were degrading culture and serious political discourse, turning literature and art into propaganda. Comfort was an absolutist in these matters, insisting that to support any government in this terrible time was to promote the debasement of politics and language. This was more or less the position Orwell himself had taken in the late 1930s, as the prospect of another war was becoming more distinct.

In 1937, Orwell published an article in the *New Statesman and Nation* in which he advocated "anti-war agitation" on these grounds:

> 1. That war against a foreign country only happens when the moneyed classes think they are going to profit from it.
>
> 2. That every war when it comes, or before it comes, is represented not as a war but as an act of self-defence against a homicidal maniac ("militarist" Germany in 1914, "Fascist" Germany next year or the year after). The essential job is to get people to recognize war propaganda when they see it, especially when it is disguised as peace propaganda.[17]

In 1938, Orwell joined the Independent Labour Party (ILP), left-wing Britain's alternative to both the Labour Party and the Communist Party of Great Britain, through which he had arranged to go to Spain as an accredited journalist and which soon after gave him entrée to the militia of the POUM (the Spanish acronym for the Worker's Party of Marxist Unification). In September, he signed an ILP manifesto headed, "If War Comes We Shall Resist It."[18]

The following March, as German troops ended the independence of Czechoslovakia, Orwell was still able to write his friend Herbert Read—poet, art critic, Britain's best-known anarchist at the time, and soon thereafter Comfort's editor and mentor at Routledge and Kegan Paul—that "war preparation" would lead to "some kind of Austro-Fascism" in Britain. Indeed, "the fascists will have it all their own way unless there is in being some body of people who are both anti-war and anti-fascist." Orwell suggested that "we lay in printing presses etc. in some discreet place" in hopes of "putting up a fight" against the coming despotism, and wondered if such figures as Roland Penrose or Bertrand Russell might put up the money to launch an underground press.[19] Earlier that year, he had even contributed a book review to *Peace News*, the antiwar organ of the pacifist Peace Pledge Union (PPU).[20]

After the German invasion of Poland ignited the war and he watched many of his literary companions enter military service, Orwell changed his mind. He resigned from the ILP, which was still advocating resistance to war, and wrote to the authorities offering to serve.[21]

He was not the only one to abruptly switch positions. A very vocal peace movement, ranging from the pacifists of the PPU to the National Peace Council and the League of Nations Union, which were antiwar and prodisarmament but not strictly pacifist, had flourished in Britain in the interwar years and actually gained strength in the 1930s as tensions in Europe increased. An estimated 150,000 to 175,000 Britons were members of one or another absolute pacifist group in 1940, many out of religious conviction. Many of these groups embraced the war, when it came, as a just struggle in defense of civilization, although some, like the Women's International League for Peace and Freedom, were torn over it. Longtime and well-known peace campaigners such as the popular philosopher, writer, and lecturer C.E.M. Joad, Labour MP Philip Noel-Baker, and Storm Jameson, the novelist and president of English PEN, publicly renounced pacifism in 1940.[22]

These were not easy decisions; they meant putting aside grave concerns about the development of war in the twentieth century that Orwell, among others, surely knew were no less valid just because the enemy was Hitler. In the final year of World War I, Brigadier General Frederick Sykes, chief of the British air staff, had prepared a study for the Allied Supreme War Council concluding that the objectives of strategic bombing were to destroy the enemy both morally and materially.[23] Doing so meant targeting industrial centers for raids that would also demoralize the civilian population. After the war, military planners of every other major power swiftly adopted a similar philosophy. Britain conducted a merciless bombing campaign against rebels in Iraq in the early 1920s, and the future Axis powers applied a similar strategy in China, Ethiopia, and Spain in the 1930s.

The interwar peace movement had gained popularity as a reaction to these events and even received mild encouragement from the British and other governments when doing so seemed politically expedient. As early as 1923, the so-called Hague Rules on Air Warfare stated that bombing was only legitimate if aimed at identifiable military objectives; otherwise, it was illegal. The agreement was never ratified, however. In March 1938, Prime Minister Neville Chamberlain condemned the bombing of civilians in Spain, stating that "the deliberate bombing of non-combatants is in all cases illegal." Later, the British Air Ministry declared nighttime bombing illegal because distinguishing military from civilian areas in the dark was nearly impossible from the air.[24]

Other military powers were drawing a different set of conclusions, however. While the combined German and Italian bombing of Guernica in April 1937, resulting in the town's destruction and hundreds of civilian deaths, had shocked the world, it succeeded in breaking the Basque regional government's resistance, enabling Franco's Nationalist forces to take the town. Hermann Göring admitted after World War II that Guernica had been a test run, and the German and Italian air forces went on to firebomb other Spanish cities.

Given these successes, many pacifists and antiwar activists feared that both sides in the new conflict would launch all-out campaigns of aerial bombardment. Shortly after the German invasion of Poland, Vera Brittain, author of the celebrated World War I autobiography *Testament of Youth* and one of England's best-known pacifists, wrote the first of her "Letters to Peace Lovers" to the country's leading newspapers, imploring the government not to bomb German cities even if the Germans bombed British population centers. "It would not help us that German women and children should join us in our agony," she wrote.[25]

Initially, such views seemed to carry some weight in Westminster. When Germany bombed Warsaw and then Rotterdam in May 1940, the government tagged the attacks

Vera Brittain, 1936.
Photo: Howard Coster, National Portrait Gallery

as examples of German barbarism; Air Minister Sir Samuel Hoare declared on the radio in April that the Royal Air Force (RAF) would never engage in such "dastardly conduct."[26]

The government was already breaking its own rule, however. In March 1940, German bombers attacked British warships off Scapa Flow in the Orkneys, killing a civilian.[27] A month later, the RAF retaliated by dropping bombs on a train station in northern Germany and, ten days later, on the occupied Norwegian capital of Oslo. One RAF flier admitted that the bombers' instruments for pinpointing targets were so inexact that "we just dropped the bombs and hoped for the best."[28] Whether the victims were military or civilian did not seem to matter much to Churchill's government, who believed fervently in air power and argued that, in any case, "demoralizing" German civilians was as important to winning the war as eliminating military targets.

Britain, locked out of Fortress Europe after the evacuation from Dunkirk, took this new kind of warfare to another level. Bombing of German cities began shortly after Hitler's troops entered the Low Countries on their way to invade France in May 1940, just as Churchill became prime minister. Almost from the first, it took the form of "area" bombing, in which the RAF deliberately targeted large areas, including whole cities, for indiscriminate attacks. No other nation had ever adopted such an approach, not even the Axis powers in Spain; the Luftwaffe's attacks on Britain never reached the same intensity.[29] Nighttime raids, which the Air Ministry had previously condemned, were now acceptable. A January 1941 British raid on Wilhelmshaven, home of much of the German fleet, created what the RAF called a "lake of fire"; by the end of the war, more than 60 percent of the city would be destroyed.[30]

These actions took place before an all-out bombing campaign was launched in February 1942. The RAF Bomber Command's first, unsuccessful attempt to wipe out a city, an assault on Cologne, took place three months later. Initially, the raids employed mainly high explosives, but soon after the Cologne attack Bomber Command began mixing in larger proportions of incendiary bombs.[31]

The most destructive incendiary attack was Operation Gomorrah against Hamburg, in July and August 1943, which ignited a fire that consumed much of the city, killing between thirty-seven thousand and forty thousand—almost as many as the entire German Blitz over England—although the final death toll will probably never be known.[32]

The February 1945 Dresden raid, which American prisoner of war Kurt Vonnegut Jr. witnessed and later made the focal point of his novel *Slaughterhouse-Five*, killed twenty-five thousand and destroyed the heart of

Dresden, February 1945: Bodies of bombing victims piled in a public square awaiting cremation. Photo: Bernd Settnik, Bundesarchiv, Bild 183-1990-0518-028

the city. Altogether, some six hundred thousand European civilians were killed and well over a million seriously injured from the British and American air raids, while 7.5 million were left homeless.[33] As much as one-third of British armaments and other war matériel went into the bombing campaign.[34]

Neither the German Blitz nor the British—and later, American—air campaigns succeeded in "demoralizing" the other side; they did not lead to defeatism, noncooperation, or a civilian uprising against the government, nor did they slow down war production significantly. But as the war advanced, bombing of civilians became a more and more deliberate policy. Indeed, what appalled Comfort—as well as many who supported the war but privately doubted the methods employed—was the language with which military command and planners discussed targeting noncombatants, despite official denials.

In a foreshadowing of the language of "shock and awe" that officials of the George W. Bush administration would use in plotting their invasion of Iraq sixty years later, British air officials in 1941 spoke of the need for "continuous blitz attacks on the densely populated workers [sic] and industrial areas," attacking "that section of the population which, in any country, is least mobile and most vulnerable to a general air attack—the working class."[35] In July 1941, Richard Peirse, head of Bomber Command, issued an order: "You will direct the main effort of the bomber force, until further instructions, toward dislocating the German transportation system, and to destroying the morale of the civilian population as a whole, and of the industrial workers in particular."[36]

That meant major population centers would be among the targets. A paper from the British Air Ministry in April had recommended the use of delayed-action bombs, "so as to prevent or seriously interfere with fire-fighting, repair and general traffic organization."[37]

At first, this was expressed mainly through internal memos, since the Air Ministry always insisted that it hit only military targets and never deliberately targeted civilian settings.[38] But within the government there was no dissembling, and as the war progressed, the tone of the conversation could not help but creep into public statements. Air Chief Marshal Arthur "Bomber" Harris, Peirse's successor as head of Bomber Command, was an outsized figure who made no secret of his hatred of Germans and showed almost complete indifference even when actions like the Dresden attack excited negative publicity.[39]

Air Chief Marshal Arthur "Bomber" Harris.
Photo: Imperial War Museum

Within a couple of years, and behind closed doors, the War Cabinet would even contemplate area attacks using mustard gas on civilians as well as military, should any evidence appear that the Germans had used poison gas on the battlefield. Churchill made it clear he approved of gas attacks against German cities. And when reports appeared in 1943 that the Germans might be planning to use biological weapons on the battlefield as a last-ditch defense, the United States set up plants to experiment with and produce such weapons as well, initiating a program that weaponized seven bioagents before it was discontinued a quarter century later.[40]

Histories of the war often cite more practical reasons than terror and punishment of civilians for the area bombing campaign—for instance, that the airborne onslaught tied down large numbers of German fighter squadrons and antiaircraft guns in the homeland, preventing Hitler from deploying them on the Russian Front. But this was not what Harris and the other British warlords argued at the time.[41]

Bombing was not the whole story, either. The British navy had imposed a tight blockade of the Nazi-occupied continent as soon as the war started. It was highly effective; within a year, it was leading to famine in German-occupied Greece, as the *New York Times* reported.[42]

Populations in occupied France as well as Germany itself were feeling the pinch, but the more severe the occupation regime and the more disfavor a group felt from the Nazis, the worse its plight. Within a couple of years, food shortages were killing thousands of Jews confined to ghettos in Warsaw and other cities. By the fall of 1941 the United States was cooperating in the blockade, and the death rate for children in the Warsaw ghetto was ten times the birth rate. Former president Herbert Hoover, who was attempting to organize food relief for occupied Europe, raged on American radio, "Is the Allied cause any further

advanced today as a consequence of this starvation of children? . . . Can you point to one benefit that has been gained
from this holocaust?"[43]*

Meanwhile, the British and French governments were
cracking down on dissidents and individuals they regarded
as suspect. Shortly after the German invasion of Poland,
the increasingly right-leaning French government began
rounding up German citizens within its borders and
sending them to concentration camps; out of some fifteen
thousand thus dealt with, about nine thousand were Jews
and most of the rest liberal enemies of Nazism.[44]

After the fall of France, in June 1940, six members of
the PPU were arrested in London and tried for creating
and putting up posters that read, "War will end when men
refuse to fight. What are YOU doing about it?"[45]

The six were eventually released. In January 1941,
Scotland Yard raided the offices of the *Daily Worker*,
and the government made it illegal to print, disseminate,
or otherwise assist in the publication of the Communist
newspaper—the same treatment meted out to *Action*, the
newspaper of Sir Oswald Mosley's pro-German British
Union of Fascists.

The *Daily Worker*'s sin was having published, in 1939,
a manifesto titled the "People's Convention for a People's
Government." It called for "defense of the people's living
standards," "adequate air raid-protection" (the government had not yet initiated any such project, despite the
growing likelihood of war), "friendship with the Soviet
Union," and "a people's peace that gets rid of the causes of
war," among other things. One of the signatories was the
actor Michael Redgrave.

In February 1941, with the German Blitz at its most
intense, Redgrave was asked to come to Broadcasting

* Hoover's anger at Churchill's policy replayed an episode during
World War I, in which his efforts to provide food relief to occupied
Belgium were opposed by then First Lord of the Admiralty Winston
Churchill, who argued that any easing would aid the German war effort.

House, where he was told of the BBC governors' decision not to employ anyone who supported the People's Convention; he was then asked to write a letter to the organizers withdrawing his support, copying the BBC. Otherwise, he would receive no new contracts to perform on the network—this despite the fact that he in no way opposed the war.

Redgrave refused and wrote to the *News Chronicle* in March, recounting the incident. In response, a number of prominent people protested, including actors Leslie Howard and Edith Evans as well as E.M. Forster and Ralph Vaughan Williams. On March 20, Churchill announced to the House of Commons that the BBC ban on Redgrave and other signatories of the People's Convention was lifted.[46]

Of course, what dissidents were experiencing in Britain was nothing next to the unparalleled tyranny the Nazi regime was imposing. Pacifists and critics of the bombing were frequently censored—even speeches in Parliament that were not on-message sometimes went unreported or underreported—and subjected to surveillance, but they were seldom prevented from holding meetings or putting out their own publications. Vera Brittain and Michael Redgrave were never imprisoned, let alone physically attacked; neither was Alex Comfort.

Contrast their treatment with a member of the German Fellowship of Reconciliation who had refused to serve in the army and was shot about the same time the PPU members were arrested.[47]

Some thirty thousand Wehrmacht soldiers were sentenced to death by German military tribunals during the war—twenty thousand of whom were executed—for crimes of desertion, "defeatism," violations of military law including attempting to rescue Jews headed for Auschwitz, and other offenses. Soon Germany would invade Russia, special units would quickly begin shooting Jews and other undesirables en masse, and the unmatched atrocity of the death camps would begin.[48]

While the RAF was punishing German cities mercilessly, British civilians were getting their share from the intense German bombing campaign that lasted from September 1940 to May 1941. The Luftwaffe dropped over fifty-seven thousand tons of high-explosive and incendiary bombs on British cities during that ten-month period, leaving more than 43,000 civilians dead and possibly as many as 139,000 injured.[49] Other parts of Europe saw much the same: in just one raid over Stalingrad in August 1941, twelve hundred planes of the advancing German forces bombed some four thousand residents of that city to their deaths.[50]

Despite the blustery and often inhumane language that British military and political leaders employed, from their perspective the RAF bombing campaign was not gratuitous but a matter of desperate necessity. Between the fall of France and the entry of the United States into the war, Britain was virtually incapable of pressing a ground offensive against Hitler. Its efforts to do so—in Crete, in Norway, in North Africa—all ended in disaster, at least initially. The only military advantages Britain retained were its air force and the fact that its fleet could still operate at will in the North Sea, the North Atlantic, and the Mediterranean.

The only way Britain could fight back, then, was to bomb German targets and blockade the Continent, hoping to gradually starve the Nazi regime or at least keep it at bay until the Americans joined the war. More precise daytime bombing of industrial targets would have been a better and more humane approach than nighttime area bombing, but, especially early in the war, British fliers lacked radar and other navigational tools that would have made this possible. Terrible as the naval blockade was, especially for the most vulnerable populations, Churchill would have been justified in arguing that backing off would allow Hitler to extend the duration of the war, perhaps by years. To directly blame Britain for starvation in the ghettos would have been completely unfair—and it is unlikely their inhabitants would have wanted Britain to end the siege, since this would have relieved pressure on Germany. The War Cabinet's strategy certainly included making the war as terrible as possible for German civilians, but it also served the military purpose

Prime Minister Churchill inspects the ruins of Coventry cathedral, November 1940. Photo: Imperial War Museum

of depriving German industry of the workforce and civil order it needed to keep the führer's armies supplied.

Germany could, of course, make the same argument. While Churchill exploited the bombing of Coventry to showcase Nazi barbarism, for example, the city was also a major center of armaments production and therefore could be considered a legitimate military target.[51]

But winning America over to the anti-Nazi crusade was the only way Britain could hope to achieve victory rather than just a stalemate with Germany. Propaganda, even when it stretched the truth, was as vital to Churchill as the RAF and the Royal Navy.

III. A PUBLIC "SET-TO"

Dissidents like Comfort were frightened by the atmosphere the war was creating at home and its effect on public consciousness. A few people spoke out, even in official circles. Former prime minister David Lloyd George in September 1940 called, unsuccessfully, for an agreement with Germany limiting bombing to "defined military objectives."[1]

In an April 1941 letter to the *Times* of London, George Bell, bishop of Chichester and a prominent figure in the Church of England, criticized strategic bombing. He continued to speak against it in the House of Lords, while two Labour MPs, Richard Stokes and Alfred Salter, attacked it steadily in the House of Commons. Bell's letter sparked a mini-rebellion, in speech and print, that had been building for some time. While the peace movement of the previous decade had died down and many of its prominent figures now supported the war, a new movement specifically opposed to nighttime bombing, bombing of civilians, and indiscriminate bombing was taking shape. When Lord Ponsonby, former Labour leader in the House of Lords, spoke against the bombing campaign in August 1940 and again in August 1941, he received a flood of letters from people who were concerned that it would reduce Britain to the moral level of the Nazis without bringing the war any closer to an end.[2]

A public pressure group, the Committee for the Abolition of Night Bombing, was founded in August 1941, succeeded the following year by the Bombing Restriction Committee. The country's largest pacifist group, the PPU, suffered no falling off of membership. From 129,289 in August 1939, it grew to 135,676 in August 1940 before dipping to 135,134 by March 1941, demonstrating that more than just a few headline names were disturbed by the government's military strategy.[3]

An April 1941 Gallup opinion poll, conducted in the midst of the Blitz, found that while 55 percent of respondents supported the RAF bombing German civilians, only 45 percent of those in London, which bore the brunt of the German fusillade, were in favor, compared to 47 percent in the city who were opposed.[4]

Those who disagreed with the government, or were disturbed by the atmosphere that was settling in, nevertheless felt increasingly isolated. Speaking to the BBC in 2004, "I don't think anyone of this generation, in this country, can appreciate what a big thing it was saying you were not going to join the war effort," said Damon Albarn, the Blur frontman and Gorillaz ringleader, whose grandfather, architect Edmund Albarn, was a "conchie"—conscientious objector—during the war. "It took an enormous amount of courage. You were basically opting out of society and had no guarantee you were ever going to be allowed back in." Edmund Albarn was stripped of his professional license for his views.[5]

Christopher Isherwood, under intense criticism for leaving Britain for America in January 1940, wrote in his diary, "Am I afraid of being bombed? Of course. Everybody is." But if he stayed, "I am afraid I should be reduced to a chattering, enraged monkey, screaming back hate at their hate."[6]

When conscientious objectors sought roles in fire brigades and ambulance services, they ran into resentment from—or on behalf of—veterans of the last war. In June 1940, the London County Council was one of more than fifty local government entities to ban employment of pacifists in all civil defense positions. (Eventually, the level of emergency and shortage of labor was such that the national government forced them to reverse themselves and accept pacifists.)[7]

The idea that bombing civilians could somehow induce them to rise against their rulers had some members of the British intelligentsia convinced, producing some quite disturbing commentary. Lord Davies, who before the war had advocated abolishing the bomber plane, wrote to one of the organizers of the Bombing Restriction Committee in 1942 that "civilians are in the fighting line and must take their medicine. . . . The more Germans that are killed, the sooner this horrible war will be over."[8] David Garnett, novelist and Bloomsbury scion, was serving as an intelligence officer. In fall 1941 he published a book entitled *The War in the Air*, in which he suggested: "By butchering the German population indiscriminately it might be possible to goad them into a desperate rising in which every member of the Nazi party would have his throat cut."[9]

Orwell himself was disturbed by some of his government's actions and the shape the British war effort was taking, but he kept his thoughts largely to himself. In 1941, he confided in his diary his feelings about the lack of self-criticism among the more patriotic English clergy. "God is asked 'to turn the hearts of our enemies, and to help us to forgive them, to give them repentance for their misdoings, and a readiness to make amends.' Nothing about our enemies forgiving *us*," he wrote.[10] Two years later, Comfort would publicly ridicule more or less the same attitude in a satirical poem in *Tribune*: "Bombs are Christian when the English drop them."

At about the same time, Orwell would write in his diary, "Two years ago, we would all have been aghast at the idea of killing civilians" in air raids—having perhaps forgotten that the RAF was already doing so by that time. When the British bound the hands of German soldiers captured during a raid on Dieppe in 1942, the Germans replied by chaining British prisoners; the British followed suit with their German captives. In his diary, Orwell noted, "The authorities in Canada have now chained up a number of German prisoners equal to the number of British prisoners chained up in Germany. What the devil are we coming to?" Orwell wrote a letter to the *Times* in which he argued that this sort of retaliation only showed that Britain was prepared to "descend . . . to the level of our enemies." He even suggested that Britain publicly refuse to retaliate against German outrages—reminiscent of Vera Brittain's earlier plea against any bombing of German population centers, even if the Germans failed to return the favor.[11]

The *Times* did not publish Orwell's letter, and, for the most part, his concerns were elsewhere. In the fall of 1941, he was asked to review Alex Comfort's first novel—curiously, the request came from the *Adelphi*, which had moved in a pacifist direction in the preceding years. *No Such Liberty* is the story of a young pathologist and his wife who flee political persecution in Nazi Germany, only to be placed in an internment camp in Britain. Their baby dies in the camp, of neglect and undernourishment. Eventually the couple are released and allowed to emigrate to the United States, but as the novel closes they are haunted by the fear that the same hysteria against political refugees will have reached America by the time they arrive.

The setting of Comfort's story would have been familiar to his readers. Some fifty-five thousand refugees from Germany, Austria, Poland, Czechoslovakia, and other parts of Europe under Nazi tutelage were in Britain in the early months of the war. Most were Jews. After the fall of France, however, MI5 began rounding up persons deemed "high security risks," and the right-wing press began campaigning to have all foreigners interned or deported, igniting a hysteria that led many employers to fire their foreign workers wholesale. "Collar them all," Winston Churchill reportedly agreed, and the government ordered all men between sixteen and sixty from Germany, Austria, or Italy interned, most of them on the Isle of Man. More than 80 percent were, or claimed to be, Jewish. Another seven thousand were sent to Canada and Australia; one boat transporting them, the *Arandora Star*, was sunk by a German U-boat, killing 714, while some of those sent to Canada were placed in a camp together with captured Nazis.[12]

The main character of *No Such Liberty*, Dr. Breitz, puts into words Comfort's apprehension that the war was driving Britain in the same direction as Nazi Germany:

> My heart sank, because I realised that the same fear was moving here as in Germany, the fear of being weak, or adhering to right principles lest they should not be an expedient, practical policy. . . . It's not that you in London are evil; it's not that the infection has gone so far that you beat and jail men, individual men, who tell you that the bacteria of your disease are there. But they are there. And I know that they must, and they will grow, till you are as we, and fear has redoubled itself.[13]

In his review, Orwell allowed that *No Such Liberty* was "a good novel as novels go at this moment," but added that it was really a "tract" written "to put forth the 'message' of pacifism." For one thing, conditions were not so very bad for refugees and were getting better: "It is not true, . . . as Mr. Comfort implies, that there is widespread spy-mania and that the prejudice against foreigners increases as the war gathers in momentum. The feeling against foreigners, which was one of the factors that made the internment of the refugees possible, has greatly died away, and Germans and Italians are now allowed into jobs that they would have been debarred from in peace-time."

Of course, Churchill's behavior had certainly suggested something like a "spy-mania." And, arguably, Orwell was implying that the democracies, the alleged bulwarks against fascism, could be excused for the terrible treatment that many refugees had received in the early period of the war simply because such treatment had relaxed, as such things tend to do. Nevertheless, Orwell posed a stark choice: "You can let the Nazis rule the world; that is evil; or you can overthrow them by war, which is also evil. There is no other choice before you. . . . We only have the chance of choosing the lesser evil and of working for the establishment of a new kind of society in which common decency will again be possible."[14]

Just a few years earlier, in *Homage to Catalonia*, his account of his experiences in the Spanish Civil War, Orwell had declared, "When I see a flesh-and-blood worker in conflict with his natural enemy, the policeman, I do not ask myself which side I am on." Yet, in attempting to address Comfort's larger concern for how the war might be changing Britain, Orwell proposed "one or two facts which underlie the structure of modern society" and which may surprise readers who have come to think of Orwell as a critic of authority:

> Civilization rests on coercion. What holds society together is not the policeman but the goodwill of common men, and yet that goodwill is powerless unless the policeman is there to back it up.... Objectively, whoever is not on the side of the policeman is on the side of the criminal, and vice versa. In so far as it hampers the British war effort, British pacifism is on the side of the

Nazis.... Objectively, the pacifist is pro-Nazi.[15]

Note that the writer who made this morally absolutist pronouncement was the same one whose fundamental objections to anarchists and pacifists included that they practice a form of "moral absolutism." What is most disturbing about Orwell's reasoning, however, is how closely it parallels that of one of his least favorite world leaders: Josef Stalin.[16]

One of the central justifications that Marxist-Leninists gave for revolution conducted and controlled by a party elite was that only this revolutionary core was in possession of the "objective" meaning of historical events—including their own actions—and the necessity that flows from them. All other parties to the struggle were misinformed or misguided, afflicted by "false consciousness."[17]

Thus, in a famous 1924 speech, "Concerning the International Situation," Stalin declared that "Social-Democracy is objectively the moderate wing of fascism" and that "'pacifism' is the strengthening of fascism with its moderate, Social-Democratic wing pushed into the forefront."[18]

The problem with this type of thinking is clear: it is always a political party or interest group or leader that decides what is "objectively" the case, and thus such thinking can change direction on command—as Communist parties around the world were bid to do when Moscow signed the Nazi-Soviet Pact, for example. But Stalin and other Communist figures, both in Russia and the West, frequently used this kind of logic against their ideological rivals, which perhaps helps explain why Comfort initially mistook Orwell for a "hard-line Marxist" when he applied it to anarcho-pacifists like Comfort.

Pacifists were an unwelcome presence during World War II, both in Britain and the United States and even among people who had once sympathized with them.

Those who refused to do service of some sort often were
imprisoned or had their movements restricted and their
publications and public statements censored. But Orwell,
given the logic he had adopted, went a critical step further,
accusing them of something like treason.

By this time Orwell was working for the BBC. A year
had passed since the Wehrmacht had defeated France,
which was now divided between the collaborationist
Vichy government in the south and an occupied northern
half that the Germans threatened to use as a staging area
for an invasion of Britain: "England is literally within
gunshot of the continent," Orwell wrote.[19]

The Lend-Lease program, under which the United
States agreed to supply weapons and other war materials to
Britain, the Free French, and the Republic of China in exchange for the use of military bases during the war, was just
beginning to enable Churchill's government to strike back
at Germany other than by air, and Hitler's invasion of Russia had cemented a wartime alliance between London and
Moscow. But the Japanese attack on Pearl Harbor was still
months away from bringing the United States into the war
on Britain's side. Britain was still isolated and embattled.

While Mosley and some eight hundred of his followers
in the prewar British Union of Fascists had been interned
after the fall of France, the British were still hearing from a
small, eccentric, but noisy group of "defeatists," some but
not all of whom were pro-German, in the fringe press and
over the airwaves from Berlin. Middleton Murry was one
of the most prominent, but this group also included the
remnants of Mosley's group; the editors of *Truth*, a right-
wing newspaper; the Duke of Bedford, a wealthy, eccentric
crypto-fascist sympathizer and pamphleteer who attempted to mediate a truce by visiting the German legation in
Dublin; and William Joyce ("Lord Haw-Haw"), a former
Mosleyite who was making propaganda broadcasts to Britain from Germany.

All of them argued that the British should dump Churchill and make peace with Hitler—whether to hold off the Soviet menace, to establish a "real" nationalist-socialist government in London, or to end the threat a long and costly war would pose to maintaining the British Empire. Roughly analogous to the America First movement active before the United States entered the war, their core argument was that Britain had nothing to gain by continuing the fight and should look to its own interests rather than to those of the French, Dutch, and other occupied nations. These individuals and factions may have been "too insignificant to be worth mentioning," Orwell wrote in one of his regular "London Letters" to *Partisan Review*, "but in this blood-stained harlequinade in which we are living one never knows what obscure individual or half-lunatic theory may not become important."[20]

Much of the Left, including the Communist Party, which had been highly critical of the government during the period of the Nazi-Soviet Pact, was now firmly behind the fight against Germany. That made it easy for pro-war leftists to deny that any real distance existed between the antiwar right and the remaining critics on the left: anarchists and pacifists such as Comfort; the poet and critic D.S. Savage; the poet and, later, crime writer Julian Symons (then a Trotskyist); Vernon Richards and Marie Louise Berneri, who ran the venerable anarchist Freedom Press and Bookshop and published the antiwar paper *War Commentary*, to which Comfort was a contributor; and George Woodcock, poet, anarchist, and editor of *NOW*, a literary journal devoted to writings that the wartime government found controversial.

There was actually a great deal of practical and ideological distance between the defeatists and the anarcho-pacifists. Many of the latter were not opposed to armed resistance to the Nazis, denounced imperialism rather than defending it, and actively opposed the right-wing nationalism that had nurtured fascism to begin with. Nor did Berlin itself regard them as allies: Vera Brittain's name would later turn up in the Gestapo's Black Book listing 2,820 people to be arrested at once if Britain was successfully invaded.[21]

But Orwell dismissed such details as irrelevant. His letter appeared in the March/April 1942 issue of *Partisan Review*, whose editors had been close to splitting over whether to support American entry into the war. Validating at least some of the concerns Comfort had highlighted in *No Such Liberty*, Orwell noted "a fresh drive against the refugees," with the British Right taking the line that "the Germans are *all* wicked, and not merely the Nazis"— mainly, he wrote, "as a way of escaping from the notion that we are fighting against fascism."

But Orwell went on to attack "pinks" he felt were either pacifists or not sufficiently pro-war. "I do seem to notice a tendency in intellectuals, especially the younger ones, to come to terms with Fascism, and it is a thing to keep one's eye on," he warned. These "quisling intellectuals," as he termed them, included Alex Comfort ("a 'pure' pacifist of the other-cheek school") and Symons, who he said "writes in a vaguely Fascist strain." He then lumped them into the same category as Middleton Murry, the Duke of Bedford, and Lord Haw-Haw and hinted, ominously, "If the Germans got to England, . . . I think I could make out at least a preliminary list of the people who would go over" to their cause.

Comfort, Symons, and other leftists opposed to the war shared none of the Right's reasons for doing so. Indeed, Orwell's only real evidence to support squeezing extreme Right and radical Left opponents of the war into the same category was that Woodcock's journal, *NOW*, had published a few pacifist pieces by the Duke of Bedford and Middleton Murry. Comfort, along with two of his closest literary allies, Woodcock and Savage, reacted to Orwell's attack by writing furious letters to *Partisan Review*. The magazine's editor, Philip Rahv, decided to publish these, along with Orwell's reply, in the September/October issue. Orwell had been unfair in yoking the pacifists to traitors like Joyce, but his respondents worked hard to outdo him.

"Orwell dislikes the French intellectuals licking up Hitler's crumbs," Savage argued, "but what's the difference between them and our intellectuals who are licking up Churchill's?" "No one in England, except Orwell and possibly the Stalinists, would think of suggesting that Julian Symons [who was Jewish] has any Fascist tendencies" wrote Woodcock, who hailed "Comrade Orwell, the former fellow-traveler of the pacifist and regular contributor to the pacifist *Adelphi*," the veteran of Spain "who returns to his old imperialist allegiances and works at the B.B.C. conducting British propaganda to fox the Indian masses!"

Comfort was just slightly more measured. "I see that Mr. Orwell is intellectual-hunting again," he wrote. Picking up on Orwell's insinuation that Britain's pacifists would make their peace with a German occupation, Comfort predicted that, under those circumstances, anarcho-pacifists like himself would, after the war, be "the only people likely to hold genuinely anti-Fascist values." It was they who would "be entrusted with the job of saving what remains of civilized values from Hitler or alternatively from Churchill," given that the Coalition Government and its allies on the left had "begun feverishly jamming into our national life all the minor pieces of Fascist practice which did not include Socialist methods."

Lashing back, Orwell denounced "the intellectual cowardice of people who are objectively and to some extent emotionally pro-Fascist, but who don't care to say so." More concretely, he objected that Comfort had exaggerated the "Fascizing processes" going on in Britain as a result of the war and vented his irritation that Woodcock had called out his involvement with the *Adelphi*. "Why not? I once wrote an article for a vegetarian paper. Does that make me a vegetarian?" he wrote, perhaps forgetting that he had criticized *NOW* for some of its occasional contributors.

Despite the fact that he personally supported the movement for Indian Home Rule, this time he even included the movement and Gandhi in his attacks, noting, "As long as twenty years ago it was cynically admitted"—he did not say by whom—"that Gandhi was very useful to the British Government. So he will be to the Japanese if they get [to India]. . . . Many, perhaps most, Indian intellectuals are emotionally pro-Japanese." This completely unfounded charge* followed fairly closely the line he and other broadcasters were directed to take by the BBC in commenting on Gandhi and the Congress Party: "The limelight should throughout be focussed . . . on the figure of Mr Gandhi, the inconsistencies of whose policy should be exposed, and who should be gradually built up as a backward-looking pacifist and Petainist . . . who has become a dangerous obstacle to the defence of India, and whose policies in fact if not in design play straight into Japanese hands."[22]

Orwell's response to Comfort was more complicated, however—at once harsher and more forgiving. "Even the work of one individual can exist at very different levels," he wrote. "For instance Mr Comfort himself has written one poem I value greatly ('The Atoll in the Mind'), and I wish he would write more of them instead of lifeless propaganda tracts dressed up as novels." But in Comfort's response to *Partisan Review*, Orwell said, Comfort had attempted to prejudice American audiences against Orwell's

---

*   Orwell was wrong. Gandhi's Quit India civil-disobedience movement, launched in August 1942, aimed at using the war to apply pressure on Britain for an immediate end to colonial rule. Gandhi and many of his allies were arrested and imprisoned, despite the fact that President Franklin Delano Roosevelt lobbied Churchill to agree to some of their demands. An Indian nationalist, Subhas Chandra Bose, raised a rebel Indian National Army with Japanese help, but Gandhi and his followers and allies had nothing to do with it.

work, misrepresented his line of thought, and indulged in intellectually dishonest propaganda. He singled out a long letter Comfort had written some weeks earlier to Cyril Connolly's new magazine, *Horizon*, as the kind of soft-headed thinking the pacifists indulged in. Comfort had written the following:

> As far as I can see, no therapy short of complete military defeat has any chance of re-establishing the common stability of literature and of the man in the street. One can imagine the greater the adversity the greater the sudden realization of a stream of imaginative work, and the greater the sudden katharsis of poetry, from the isolated interpretation of war as calamity to the realization of the imaginative and actual tragedy of Man. When we have access again to the literature of the war years in France, Poland and Czechoslovakia, I am confident that that is what we shall find.[23]

Or, as he later summarized his argument: "Adversity tended to produce great literature."[24]

Comfort had written his original letter in answer to an essay by Spender arguing that the younger poets had not responded adequately to the war.[25] Did Comfort believe a Nazi victory would have a stimulating effect on the arts? Nothing less than "money-sheltered ignorance" could cause one to believe that "literary life is still going on, for instance, in Poland," Orwell wrote. What more proof was needed that "our English pacifists are tending toward active pro-Fascism"?

Reading more closely, Comfort was clearly not encouraging a Nazi victory in his *Horizon* piece. He was not talking so much about the war, in fact, as the prospects for literature in a wartime culture defined by a fog of propaganda and official lies. He could certainly be accused of ignoring, for argument's sake, the qualitative differences between the Nazi regime and the capitalist democracies, however corrupt and oppressive the latter were. But he saw his wartime "job" differently from how someone like Orwell did. In a 1943 letter to *Tribune*—a newspaper Orwell would soon join as literary editor—Comfort wrote, "It seems to me that a particular responsibility belongs to the English writers and artists. They, at least, pretend to value both life and culture internationally. There are times when denunciation is a moral and an aesthetic duty. The present seems to me to be one such, and I invite other writers who share my feeling to say so publicly and as soon as possible."[26]

Comfort used the word "responsibility" in a particular and often ironic way throughout his political writings. As he explained in a postwar BBC radio talk, responsibility was both "a positive duty to remember that you are a human being, and a negative duty of disobedience to irrational and anti-human instructions."[27]

It was those who obeyed, who played the part of good citizens and subjects in a time of crisis, who were irresponsible and who, wittingly or not, promoted a return to "barbarism"—another term that Comfort used in a special sense, as any system, like fascism, that attempts "to summate the destructive influences and use them as a basis for a society."[28]

A Quaker publication in 1940 had stated that the purpose of antiwar activity during the war was to create a base of support for a "new nonviolent society" after the war was over.[29] The task of artists and writers, Comfort believed, was to create a culture of resistance that could challenge the even more powerful, more efficiently oppressive states that were likely to arise out of the war; the best way to begin was to challenge his government now, while the war was still being fought.

But even if Comfort and his comrades really were not "emotional" fascists, what irritated Orwell was their

seeming refusal to say how they would go about ridding
the world of Hitler if the British, American, and Soviet
states were not to play a role and their persistent hammer-
ing on the shortcomings of their own government. "In the
circumstances," he wrote of the terrifying period just after
the fall of France and the English retreat to Dunkirk,

> all one could do was to "support" the war, which in-
> volved supporting Churchill, and hope that in some
> way it would all come right on the night—i.e. that the
> mere necessities of war, the inevitable drift toward a cen-
> tralized economy and a more equal standard of living,
> would force the regime gradually to the Left and allow
> the worst reactionaries to be levered out.... Revolution-
> ary defeatism, or anything approaching it, is nonsense in
> our geographical situation. If there were even a week's
> serious disorganization in the armed forces the Nazis
> would be here, after which one might as well stop talking
> about revolution.[30]

Orwell hoped, at least faintly, that the government-directed
wartime economy would become a stepping-stone to
socialism, the overthrow of the class system, and the mar-
ginalization of the Right. Symons, who later became close
to Orwell, summed up his friend's perspective this way: "It
was necessary for the war to be fought, with Socialism the
end to be achieved when it had been won." Comfort and
the other anarcho-pacifists were far more cynical. Who
were the people directing the war effort? they asked. What
were their aims, and why should people on the left suddenly trust them?

Just a few short years earlier, many of the same
crew—minus Churchill—had tacitly supported the fascist insurgency in Spain. Anthony Eden, Churchill's
dashing foreign secretary, while serving in the same post
under Stanley Baldwin's government, had formulated a

nonintervention policy for Britain and France in 1937 that effectively isolated the Republican government in Madrid while giving Hitler and Mussolini free rein to back Franco's insurgency.*

Lord Halifax, Eden's successor, was an arch-appeaser who had that same year congratulated Hitler, declaring that the führer had "performed a great service for Germany [by] preventing the entry of communism into his own country."[31]

The British government had been exceedingly cautious about admitting Jewish refugees attempting to flee Nazi Germany, either to England or Palestine, and quick to treat many of them as enemy aliens once the war began. Apologetics for Hitler's regime were common in respectable Britain before the war, some centered on accusations that the Jews had helped bankroll the Bolsheviks.[32]

Even Churchill had openly admired Mussolini's fascism—"the ultimate means of protection against the cancerous growth of Bolshevism"—for many years, until the Italian dictator climbed into bed with Hitler.[33] Churchill had already written his own chapter in the history of wartime atrocity while serving as colonial secretary in 1920, having ordered poison gas to be used against rebels in British-held Iraq ("Bomber" Harris cut his teeth devising aerial assaults in that campaign). Like so much of the British governing class, Churchill was a passionate opponent of home rule for India, where outrage over the Amritsar massacre of 1919, in which more than fifteen hundred peaceful protesters and religious pilgrims were gunned down by British troops, was still fresh in the minds of millions.

And so a strong whiff of hypocrisy clung to a British ruling class who suddenly were billing themselves as the leaders of an antifascist crusade. "It was impossible not to be paranoid about the glibness of the conversion," Comfort,

---

*   Eden resigned early the following year, realizing—too late—that nonintervention would not work and that Germany and Italy would never abide by an agreement to respect Spain's territorial integrity.

still palpably outraged by their behavior, wrote in a 1983 essay for a collection on Orwell and *Nineteen Eighty-Four*. "What were all those old British acquaintances of Ribbentrop in high places, suddenly spouting anti-fascist rhetoric, really up to? It was as if Jerry Falwell were to open a Christian abortion clinic—unbelievable."[34]

Orwell himself was fully aware that, under somewhat different circumstances, many of the people leading the war effort could have aligned themselves with the fascist regimes, even offering a bill of charges against them in an article for *Tribune* published not long after he left the BBC.[35]

But he did so to clear the decks for an attack on the Left, later in the same piece, for "the same tendency to excuse almost anything 'because they're on our side'" when it came to the Soviets. Other than occasionally voicing vague hopes for a libertarian-socialist revolution, he seems never to have thought through the implications of allowing Churchill and his companions to lead the nation in its fight against the very regimes many of them had tolerated before the war.

Comfort and other dissidents did not dismiss the issue so casually: What was the elite's real purpose in going to war? To liberate France? To end the fascist grip on most of Europe? Or to establish their own hegemony? To jump-start development of a new generation of super-weapons? To eliminate any threat to the Empire, including India? To suppress dissent at home and, perhaps, give Germany just enough room to smash the Soviet Union before Britain (and, eventually, the United States) invaded the Continent and dictated a new order there? Other explanations might do, but to leave unasked these questions about people the Left, including Orwell, had criticized harshly just a few years earlier seemed, to someone like Comfort, naive.

IV. A DISAGREEMENT IN VERSE

The *Partisan Review* exchange had taken a nasty, personal turn, but between the time Comfort replied to Orwell's original article and Orwell wrote his retort, the two had a respectful private exchange of letters. In response to a query from Comfort, Orwell explained some references he had made to "Jew-baiting of a mild kind" in the pages of the *Adelphi*, and Comfort admitted to being more uneasy about his perceived proximity to defeatists like Middleton Murry than he had let on in print. *Peace News*, the anti-war organ of the PPU, which Middleton Murry was now editing, was not fascist, Comfort wrote, but "was trying, as you say, to get away with both ends of the same argument. . . . I have written a commination [denunciation] to J. M. Murry but he did not print it."*

Comfort went on to compliment Orwell on his much-admired essay in *Horizon* on smutty postcards, "The Art of Donald McGill," and even thanked him for his negative review of *No Such Liberty*: "I'd like to have started an argument over that review of yours, but the *Adelphi* hadn't room to unleash me. Anyhow, thank you for doing it. It made me revise several ideas."[1]

---

*   No such document appears to have survived.

There is much in Comfort's letter about what he would like to have done to address Orwell's arguments in print but for various reasons was unable to. And it is possible he initiated the exchange partly for another reason: to promote his and the other New Romantics' poetry. In *Partisan Review*, Orwell had mentioned liking "An Atoll in the Mind," one of Comfort's strongest early poems. Orwell had become aware of it in March, when Herbert Read, appearing on one of Orwell's broadcasts, discussed and presented the work of some of the New Romantics. He closed by reading "An Atoll in the Mind," whose last two stanzas use trees as a metaphor for the two futures that could grow out of, or alongside, the war's orgy of death:

> But when on the island's whaleback spring green blades
> new land over water wavers, birds bring seeds
> and tides plant slender trunks by the lagoon
>
> I find the image of the mind's two trees cast downward,
> one tilting leaves to catch the sun's bright pennies,
> one dark as water, rooted among the bones.

The poem, which Stephen Spender singled out in a roundup of the poetry scene in *Horizon*, was included in Comfort's first substantial collection, *A Wreath for the Living*, which Read brought out from Routledge that fall.[2] Comfort, meanwhile, had virtually taken over editing *Poetry Quarterly*, published by Grey Walls Press, turning it into a showcase for the New Romantics and other younger poets. He also launched his own little magazine, *Poetry Folios*, which he would coedit until 1947. Following his exchange with Orwell, he was also bombarding *Partisan Review* with material that he and some of his New Romantic allies had written.

While Orwell's BBC broadcasts to India reached tiny audiences—only 121,000 Indians out of some 300 million actually owned radios[3]—by this time he was attracting some

of the most prominent names in literary Britain to partici-
pate, including T. S. Eliot, E. M. Forster, Edmund Blunden,
and Dylan Thomas; shortly after the *Partisan Review* fracas,
he invited Woodcock to take part as well.[4] It made sense,
then, for Comfort to cultivate Orwell, and Comfort had
reason to think he could win the broadcaster's support.

Late in the year, Comfort and the poet John Bayliss
hatched the idea of putting out a book-length annual including some of the best material from Grey Walls along

Broadcasting to India on the BBC. Standing (l to r): George Woodcock,
Mulk Raj Anand, George Orwell, William Empson. Seated (l to r):
Herbert Read, Edmund Blunden. Photo: British Broadcasting Corporation

with other poetry and prose they solicited from outside the
New Romantic circle. Among the contributors they ap-
proached was Orwell, who submitted his essay, "Looking
Back on the Spanish War."

When the piece, one of his finest, appeared "in muti-
lated form" in Comfort and Bayliss's volume, *New Road
1943*, Orwell complained to Dwight Macdonald.[5] They had
included only the first three sections and the seventh section of the piece, which dwell mostly on Orwell's personal
experiences and sorrow over the demise of the Spanish
Revolution. They left out the sections in which he offered
his political analysis from the vantage point of the global conflict that succeeded it, although they summarized it
briefly in an editors' note. In those sections, Orwell wrote
that, in wartime, "There is always the temptation to say:
'One side is as bad as the other. I am neutral.' In practice,
however, one cannot be neutral, and there is hardly such a
thing as a war in which it makes no difference who wins.
Nearly always one side stands more or less for progress,
the other more or less for reaction."[6]

Comfort, of course, took exactly the opposite stance.
Yet when he sent Orwell a copy of *New Road*, Orwell said
nothing to him about the editing. Instead, he praised the
"general level of the verse you have got together," adding
that "I should think half the writers were not known to
me before." He said he would try to get Forster to discuss *New Road* in one of the monthly book talks to India
that Orwell had arranged for him to give—which Forster
did, on August 7. "There is no sales value there," Orwell
told Comfort, "but it extends your publicity a little and by
talking about these things on the air in wartime one has the
feeling that one is keeping a tiny lamp alight somewhere."

Noting that *New Road* included a contribution by
J.M. Tambimuttu, the Sri Lankan poet and publisher of
another influential little magazine, *Poetry London*, Orwell
suggested that Comfort include "some other Indians" in

future editions as a way to help promote "decent cultural relations between Europe and Asia."[7]

A few weeks later, Orwell wrote Comfort that he would be sending him two short stories by the Indian writer Prem Chand for the next edition of *New Road*: "I am rather disappointed with them, at any rate they are not as good as the one which was in that Indian review I told you about, but you might care to have a look at them."[8]

Orwell also made a partial apology to Comfort: "I am afraid I was rather rude to you in our *Tribune* set-to, but you yourself weren't altogether polite to certain people." Orwell was referring to a vitriolic exchange, in verse form, that they had just launched against each other in the newspaper. On June 4, Comfort published "Letter to an American Visitor," a fifteen-stanza poem in ottava rima, the Italian form that Byron had perfected as a satiric weapon in the early nineteenth century. Replete with references to Horace's *Ars Poetica* and other classical sources, the poem itself is partly patterned after Byron's "The Vision of Judgment," a satire on the poet laureate Robert Southey's grandiose commemorative poem of the same title, addressed to the late King George III. The model was appropriate, since Byron's annoyance at Southey stemmed from the fact that the laureate was a former radical who had once written a tribute to the medieval peasant rebel Wat Tyler.

Comfort may have been inspired to write and submit his poem to *Tribune* by a poem his friend and fellow New Romantic Nicholas Moore had published in the paper a week earlier, titled "That Monstrous Man," in which Moore argued that Britain was committing many of the same crimes it was allegedly trying to prevent the Germans from perpetrating. Comparing his country to "a charming girl" being roughly handled by "foreign hands," he wrote,

> You have forgotten that she was star of stars,
> Have pulled her down to meet the grand demand

Of your monstrous and indelicate war.
Denials are no use. Now once again
To save her beauty you have caused it pain,
And to yourself have proved that monstrous man.

Orwell had been struck by Moore's poem, cutting it out and pasting it in his wartime diary.[9] Comfort's poem was longer and attacked more specific targets. Addressed to a fictional "Columbian poet"—that is, an American poet—who had recently returned from Britain, it was an uninhibited attack on Churchill and his War Cabinet ("pimps in hardware coronets"), the BBC ("bookie, pimp and vet"), and the artists and writers who had signed on to support and propagandize the war effort.*

You met them all. You don't require a list
    Of understrapping ghosts who once were writers—
Who celebrate the size of Britain's fist,
    Write notes for sermons, dish out pep to mitres,
    Fake letters from the Men who Fly our Fighters,
Cheer when we blast some enemy bungalows—
    Think up atrocities, the artful blighters,
To keep the grindstone at the public's nose—
    Combining moral uplift and pornography,
    Produced with arty paper and typography.[10]

Verse after verse ridiculed Churchill's stirring speeches as "the dim productions of his bulldog brain," reviled the church's willingness to preach "that bombs are Christian when the English drop them," and insinuated that Britain's literary giants were willing to turn out propaganda in exchange for avoiding military service.

*   Peter Davison, editor of Orwell's *Complete Works*, noted, "There have been many guesses as to who the visiting American was. In a letter giving the editors permission to reprint the poem, Alex Comfort revealed that 'the visitor was imaginary' (1 August 1995)" (*Complete Works*, 15:141).

Comfort could be gratuitously cruel to his perceived enemies, and he aimed an especially mean jab at the poet Louis MacNeice, who was well known in the United States and had joined the BBC about the same time as Orwell to produce cultural programs designed to strengthen American identification with the British cause. One of MacNeice's scripts touched on the Nazis' murderous policies toward people with physical and intellectual disabilities, invoking his younger brother William, who had Down syndrome, for heart-tugging effect. This was too much for Comfort.

> I shan't forgive Macneice his crippled brother
>> Whom just a year ago on New Year's Day
>> The Germans murdered in a radio play.

By contrast, Comfort paused briefly to defend MacNeice's friend Auden, who had been reviled for moving to the United States after the war began:

> Out of the looney-bin, they say,
> A quiet place where men with minds could write.

Notably, Comfort's poem left Orwell alone. In fact, Comfort never attacked Orwell's cultural broadcasts as propaganda, even though they were not that different in intent from MacNeice's. They did indeed serve as window dressing for the British overlords' wartime repression of the Congress Party and imprisonment of its leaders. Neither did Comfort attack his friends Read and Woodcock for participating in Orwell's programs. This may simply reflect the fact that they were not broadcast in Britain, so Comfort never actually heard them. It is also possible that, since Orwell sometimes featured the poetry of Comfort and the other New Romantics, Comfort regarded him as too valuable a literary ally to abuse in print.

Comfort could hardly complain that the wartime

censors were silencing him—at least not yet: Aneurin Bevan, one of the great figures of the Labour Party, was editor of *Tribune* at the time and hadn't vetoed the inclusion of "Letter to an American Visitor." However, Comfort took the precaution of using an assumed name, "Obadiah Hornbooke," and the editors were good enough to supply the following footnote: "In fairness to 'Mr. Hornbooke,' it should be stated that he was willing to sign his name if we insisted, but preferred a pseudonym." Comfort had landed a few justified blows, but he had come disturbingly close to dismissing the unprecedented atrocities the Germans were committing and impugning the motives of many artists and writers who were working hard and without much reward to defeat fascism.

Two weeks later, on June 18, Orwell—under his own name—responded in *Tribune* with his own Byronic satire, "As One Non-Combatant to Another (A letter to 'Obadiah Hornbooke')." Orwell decried a poet—unmistakably Comfort—

> strutting from the sandbagged portal
> Of that small world where barkers ply their art,
> And each new "school" believes itself immortal,
> Just like the horse that draws the knacker's cart;
> O captain of a clique of self-advancers,
> Where slogans serve for thought and sneers for answers—
> You've chosen well your moment to appear
> And hold your nose amid a world of horror
> Like Dr. Bowdler walking through Gomorrah.

"Your hands are clean, and so were Pontius Pilate's," Orwell went on, before accusing Comfort of enjoying life on the sidelines without "even a libel action" while benefiting from the sacrifice of others in the war against Hitler. Orwell hastened to deny he was one of Churchill's promoters, but argued that the prime minister was the necessary leader at the time:

> I've no wish to praise him,
> I'd gladly shoot him when the war is won,
> Or now, if there was someone to replace him
> But unlike some, I'll pay him what I owe him.

The heart of the poem, however, is an almost anguished attempt to justify his own decision to offer his services and his reputation to a government he knew was trafficking in lies and propaganda, and to distinguish himself from the professional liars.

> Your chief target is the radio hack,
> The hired pep-talker—he's a safe objective,
> Since he's unpopular and can't hit back.
> It doesn't need the eye of a detective
> To look down Portland Place and spot the whores,
> But there are men (I grant, not the most heeded)
> With twice your gifts and courage three times yours
> Who do that dirty work because it's needed;
> Not blindly, but for reasons they can balance,
> They wear their seats out and lay waste their talents.

> All propaganda's lying, yours or mine;
> It's lying even when the facts are true;
> That goes for Goebbels or the "party line,"
> Or the Primrose League* or P.P.U.
> But there are truths that small lies can serve,
> And dirtier lies that scruples can gild over;
> To waste your brains on war may need more nerve
> Than to dodge facts and live in mental clover;
> It's mean enough when other men are dying,
> But when you lie, it's much to know you're lying.

*   An organization, cofounded by Churchill's father, that promoted Conservative Party principles.

Almost incredibly, after this outburst, the poem ends on a friendly note. Orwell was always suspicious of saintly figures—although he would be elevated into one after his death—and he urged Comfort not to set himself apart from principled antifascists who would welcome his help in the fight against Hitler.

> For the half-way saint and cautious hero,
> Whose head's unbloody even if "unbowed,"
> My admiration's near to zero;
> So my last words would be: Come off that cloud,
> Unship those wings that hardly dared to flitter,
> And spout your halo for a pint of bitter.

The Hornbooke/Orwell exchange made a lasting impression on Philip Larkin, who included it in his 1973 *Oxford Book of Twentieth-Century English Verse*. Curiously, it also brought the combatants closer together, first by renewing Orwell's respect for Comfort's poetic gift. "As a piece of verse your contribution was immensely better, a thing most of the people who spoke to me about it hadn't noticed," he wrote to Comfort soon after. "I think no one noticed that your stanzas had the same rhyme going right the way through. There is no respect for virtuosity nowadays."[11]

But there were also signs that, despite the anger he expressed in his poem, he was considering Comfort's views on art, literature, and the war more carefully. "I have thought over what you have said about the reviving effect of defeat upon literature and also upon national life," he wrote. "I think you may well be right, but it seems to me that such a revival is only against something, ie. against foreign oppression, and can't lead beyond a certain point unless that oppression is ultimately to be broken, which must be by military means. I suppose however one might accept defeat in a mystical belief that it will ultimately break down of its own accord."[12]

It was easier, perhaps, for Orwell's thoughts to turn in this direction in the summer of 1943, when the German army was being driven, agonizingly, from Russia and the Allied invasion of occupied Europe was in the planning stage. A German invasion of England had become an improbability, and rebuilding a culture from the ashes of defeat and occupation was something to be observed on the Continent, not in the British Isles. Additionally, Orwell was clearly tired of defending his decision to work for the government. Two months later, he resigned from the BBC "after wasting 2 years in it." In a letter to a friend, he confided, "Re cynicism, you'd be cynical yourself if you were in this job. . . . Then by some time in 1944 I might be near-human again & able to write something serious. At present I'm just an orange that's been trodden on by a very dirty boot."[13]

While Orwell was reconsidering his attitude toward service on behalf of the government,* Comfort was busy clarifying his ideas about war and resistance in the face of criticism from Orwell and others. Comfort took a some-times dim view of conscientious objectors, some of whom, rather than offering real opposition or serious critique of war, simply signed on as medics, as orderlies, or in some other noncontroversial role. His thinking came together in a novel he completed just as the "*Tribune* set-to" was ending; it would be published in 1944 as *The Power House*.

Comfort wrote the novel partly in Dublin, where he had been sent for several months to receive midwife training—because, he noted years later, London hospitals were not able to provide it during the war and not enough women at the time were having children there—and partly back in London while serving as a volunteer firewatcher. He composed much of it on a portable typewriter that

---

* The BBC was, and is, a quasi-autonomous public-service corporation operating under a royal charter and thus is not government-owned. During the war, however, it was wholly committed to supporting the war effort.

folded in two, in a community center across the street from the Royal London Hospital that served as a shelter during air raids. There, he said, his attention was occasionally distracted by a group of men who whiled away the time boxing.[14]

The novel, which bears a family resemblance to Hemingway's *For Whom the Bell Tolls*, follows a group of French soldiers from the disastrous early days of the German invasion through the retreat from the Belgian frontier to Paris and their attempts to forge an underground resistance built on acts of assassination and sabotage, some successful and some not. It culminates in an attempt to blow up an electrical plant. The book was Comfort's most ambitious to date, and it divided critics; some judged it extraordinary while others, even some who were politically sympathetic, found the narrative too grim and opaque to finish. Many readers—including in France, where it was translated and widely praised—were impressed by Comfort's ability to conjure the world of the French Resistance, of which he knew nothing firsthand. Indeed, he'd only been in the country once, as a boy, although he knew the language well.[15]

The Power House is a novel of ideas, although it contains a great deal of detailed physical description, and Comfort wrote it in part to address the charge of defeatism in the face of German occupation. But he may have found his subject in something Orwell himself suggested. In a January 29, 1942, broadcast, Orwell had called attention to the role of sabotage by workers and members of the anti-Nazi Resistance. "Every time a piece of machinery is wrecked or an ammunition dump mysteriously catches fire," he said, "precautions have to be redoubled. . . . When Hitler finally falls, the European workers who idled, shammed sickness, wasted material and damaged machinery in the factories, will have played an important role in his destruction."[16]

Comfort took this idea considerably farther. Just because he opposed war did not mean he opposed violence against oppressive regimes. In *The Power House*, he clearly sides with the Maquis—the French Resistance to the German occupation—seeing in this indigenous movement not just an assist to the British war against Hitler but an alternative. Whichever side won, Comfort argued,

The Power House (1st UK edition).
Courtesy Nicholas Comfort

the result would be new and more refined methods of destruction, death, and political domination—if not by the Germans then by the Americans, the British, and the Soviets.

The homegrown Resistance—in France, Yugoslavia, Greece, and elsewhere—depended heavily for supplies and support on the British and Americans, a fact not mentioned in the novel. Yet these movements held out the possibility not just of defeating Hitler but of nurturing a new and freer society by organizing outside the boundaries of the State. Orwell, who devoted considerable time during the war to his duties in the Home Guard, at least partially agreed. "Already people are spontaneously forming local defense squads, and hand-grenades are probably being manufactured by amateurs," he wrote in his diary, hopefully, in the months after the fall of France.[17]

A few months after their exchange in *Tribune*, Orwell left the BBC to become the paper's literary editor. Aiming to widen its array of voices, he wrote letters of invitation to Eliot, Treece, and Comfort, among others. "Of course I can't undertake in advance to print anything but would always read anything of yours with interest," Orwell wrote Comfort, although "we can't undertake to print direct pacifist propaganda." That said, "I should like very much if you could do another satirical poem."[18]

It took some months, but Comfort published another poem in *Tribune* the following June, titled, with a slight change in the spelling of the alleged author's last name, "The Little Apocalypse of Obadiah Hornbrook." Again he satirized wartime propagandists: "Where are the writers?" "All around you, look— / Peddling democracy like pigs in clover." The poem imagines Wordsworth coming back to life and nearly being recruited to deliver broadcasts by the BBC. Almost in passing, it touches on a far more serious matter: the Allies' deliberate bombing of civilian population centers. "We need some pens to help us peddle fetters," Hornbrook tells Wordsworth. "Cheer like a sport when Hamburg slums get pasted."[19]

Writers on both sides of the Atlantic knew perfectly well what they were endorsing when they championed the war, Comfort charged, while the dissidents saw their work ignored.

> "America?" "MacLeish is going strong,
>   Teaching the others how to like the stink
> Of putrefaction, mixing Right and Wrong
>   Like apple pie and cream, or turd and ink,
> Helping the bloodstained caravan along,
>   Teaching the cannon-fodder what to think
>   (I ought to warn you, though, not to hobnob
>   With Kenneth Patchen, or you'll lose your job.)..."*

Comfort's poem elicited some furious letters, most of them expressing anger that *Tribune* would publish such an attack. Orwell responded, first reassuring the paper's readers that he did not agree with "Hornbrook," then adding that there were lines the editors would not cross: "We wouldn't print an article in praise of antisemitism, for instance. But granted the necessary minimum of agreement, literary merit is the only thing that matters."

Orwell went a bit further in defending Comfort, however. "I should be the last to claim that we are morally superior to our enemies," he wrote, "and there is quite a strong case for saying that British imperialism is actually worse than Nazism." Certainly, there was more freedom

---

*   The fortunes of these two American poets could not have been more different. Archibald MacLeish, who was librarian of Congress from 1939 to 1944, was also a war propagandist as director of the War Department's Office of Facts and Figures and assistant director of the Office of War Information. He went on to a professorship at Harvard University after the war. Kenneth Patchen, a more unconventional poet, was an outspoken pacifist during the war; he remained a cult figure and struggled financially for most of his life. He and Comfort became friends, and Comfort helped raise money to support him in succeeding decades.

of expression in "the blackest patches of the British Empire" than in the totalitarian countries, but "I want that to remain true. And by sometimes giving a hearing to unpopular opinions, I think we help it to do so."[20]

This was during the last year of the war, when the German defeat was only a matter of time. By then, Orwell was less concerned about pro-Nazi fifth columnists than Soviet apologists in Britain and America, whom he feared would weaken the democracies' resolve against Stalin. On this topic, he could be just as righteous as Comfort. "Willingness to criticise Russia and Stalin" is "*the* test of intellectual honesty," he wrote in an August 1944 letter to Middleton Murry in which he took the one-time apologist for Nazism to task for "the very tender way in which you have handled Stalin and his regime" in the *Adelphi*. "The thing that needs courage is to attack Russia, the only thing that the greater part of the British intelligentsia now believe in."[21]

In his *Tribune* column, Orwell went farther: "Do remember that dishonesty and cowardice always have to be paid for. Don't imagine that for years on end you can make yourself the boot-licking propagandist of the Soviet regime, or any other regime, and then suddenly return to mental decency. Once a whore, always a whore."[22]

Perhaps so—but how far was one allowed to go in criticizing the postwar order that America, Britain, and their allies were busy creating before being branded a "boot-licking" Soviet apologist? Orwell left very little room for writers who were more concerned about their own government's behavior than about ritually denouncing Stalin, and he had no patience for comparisons between West and East that didn't favor the former, even if the aim was simply to keep Western governments from adopting their own brand of repression. He had an exaggerated view of the influence Moscow exercised over British intellectuals, his friend Woodcock concluded, and that prompted him to find the Soviet Union's tentacles even where they weren't.[23]

In 1946, still in the first year of the postwar Labour Government, Orwell speculated in one of his London Letters to *Partisan Review* that "'underground' Communist M.P.s—that is, M.P.s elected as Labour men but secretly members of the C.P. or reliably sympathetic to it"—numbered twenty or thirty out of more than three hundred Labour members.[24] As we will see, however, he was never able to identify more than two or three.

Plenty of reasonable people disagreed. In 1940, Louis MacNeice—whom Comfort would cruelly attack in print a couple of years later—wrote in a letter to the left-of-center American monthly *Common Sense*, "You will want to know about the Intellectual Front (I use this Stalinesque phrase deliberately). Well, there is no front." Most intellectuals in Britain aligned with the Labour Party, which, MacNeice opined, "is really more committed to winning the war than the Conservatives."[25]

V. COMMON GROUND

Orwell, of course, had personal experience to back up his fears. Following his return from Spain, where he had come close to being arrested, imprisoned, and possibly killed by the Soviet-backed Republican authorities, some of his articles were censored or rejected by pro-Soviet editors at the *News Chronicle* and the *New Statesman*. Later, working at the BBC, he knew that following the German invasion of Russia the network had adopted a wartime policy of downplaying any negative news or commentary about the Soviet regime.[1]

This extended to other parts of the cultural establishment. In 1944, he faced great trouble getting *Animal Farm* published, partly due to the discomfort some British houses felt at underwriting a thinly veiled denunciation of Stalin. Orwell's longtime publisher, Gollancz, rejected the book on political grounds. T. S. Eliot's house, Faber and Faber, turned it down as well. Eliot explained in a convoluted letter to Orwell that "we have no conviction . . . that this is the right point of view from which to criticise the political situation at the present time."[2]

Finally, Orwell sent the manuscript to Secker and Warburg, which had a reputation for taking chances with socialist texts and which had published *Homage to Catalonia* in 1938; the firm issued his political fable in August 1945. Two years after the book appeared, he heard a report that fifteen hundred copies of a Ukrainian edition of *Animal Farm* had been seized by the American authorities in Munich and handed over to Soviet functionaries working to repatriate their nationals still in Germany after the war.[3]

Orwell wasn't only an anti-Stalinist, however, and as the war wound down, he grew more concerned about the very things Comfort had been warning of but which he himself had been inclined to dismiss: the degree to which wartime intolerance of dissent in Britain was becoming institutionalized and the extent to which public intellectuals were willing, even happy, to comply. Most of the British intelligentsia were "perfectly ready for dictatorial methods, secret police, systematic falsifications of history, etc.," Orwell wrote in a letter to his friend W. J. Willmett shortly before D-Day.[4]

At about the same time, in his *Tribune* column, he noted, "The MoI [Ministry of Information] does not, of course, dictate a party line or issue an *index expurgatorius*. It merely 'advises.' And though there is no definite prohibition, no clear statement that this or that must not be printed, official policy is never flouted. Circus dogs jump when the trainer cracks his whip, but the really well-trained dog is the one that turns his somersault when there is no whip."[5]

Orwell suggested no solution to this dilemma, but for Comfort the next step was to protest as vocally as possible. In January 1944, a few months before Orwell wrote these words and at a time when the Allied bombing of German cities was escalating, Comfort sent a letter to the subscribers of *Poetry Folios*, and to other luminaries of the British artistic and literary world, making the following appeal:

> Many people who have an interest as artists in cultural
> and human values are disquieted at our present bombing

policy. I have drawn up a declaration and protest in the hope that a larger number of people in the categories of writers, artists and musicians, all specially concerned with the values of cultural life and civilisation, may be willing to add their signatures and so increase the effectiveness of the memorial. I enclose a copy of the proposed wording herewith, and beg you to unite with other signatories.

The declaration itself was short and blunt:

We the undersigned regard with growing disquietude the wanton destruction of civilian life and national culture by the Government's policy of aerial bombardment, which seems to us to imitate in an aggravated form the example of the Germans. We do not accept the denials issued by the Government of the charge that such bombardment is indiscriminate; and we feel it to be our duty as writers, artists and musicians to protest against it in the strongest possible terms, as an offence against humanity.

The declaration endorsed a recent appeal by the International Red Cross Committee to all belligerent powers to halt "methods of warfare that affect civilian lives" and protested that "the principles of international law for the protection of lives and property are being relegated more and more to the background in favor of the unreserved pursuit of total warfare."

The response to Comfort's solicitation was enthusiastic. While a few of his friends, such as Spender, declined to endorse it ("I am a coward, obviously, in this choice," he wrote back),[6] the names he gathered and released in support of the declaration included Benjamin Britten and Peter Pears, Vera Brittain, Clifford Curzon, the novelist and memoirist Denton Welch, playwright Laurence Housman, and poet James Kirkup, along with Comfort's friends and allies Read, Savage, and Woodcock. Despite the caliber of the signatories, the declaration failed to attract much attention, and what there was tended to be unsympathetic. "To the piffling minority of Britons who object to Allied bombings as 'an offence against humanity' were added 26 names last week," the weekly *News Review* reported sneeringly on March 23—but then listed all the names, along with a description of each individual, suggesting that the paper didn't consider their protest such a minor affair after all.

While Orwell largely dug into his work as *Tribune* literary editor, Comfort was becoming more and more outspoken. In October, he published an article in Woodcock's magazine, *NOW*, in which he denounced conscription while placing much of the responsibility for the war's horrors on writers and intellectuals who dared not speak out. "*Horizon* is full of gratitude that through four years of war not one word has been censored," he complained. "Who the mischief wants to censor it? . . . Everyone enjoys freedom provided they do not use it responsibly." As for the politicians, "it has been an article of pride . . . that the public would shove its head into any old noose they might show it—obedience and an absence of direct action." The people "learn slowly and incompletely," he wrote, but he cherished the hope that before the next war broke out, they would precipitate their leaders "into the filth where they deserve to be."[7]

While Orwell was at the BBC, Comfort's poetry was occasionally heard over the Indian service, but with these latest sallies, things changed. Earlier in October, the network's head of European productions, W.P. Rilla, had written to Comfort asking to discuss with him a series of broadcasts to the Continent, much of which was now in the process of being liberated from the Nazis, about "the current English literary scene." Rilla wanted to know whether Comfort would make a recording to be used in the series and asked for his views on a list of additional proposed contributors that was attached to the letter.[8]

Since Orwell's departure, Comfort had noticed that the political spectrum in the BBC's cultural programming was narrowing—a change he saw reflected in Rilla's list. He shot back a letter noting that the proposed discussion seemed to be confined to "acquiescent writers" and asking if his name had been included on a "black list" within the BBC. Rilla wrote back immediately, assuring him that "I was completely unaware that any discrimination against your broadcasting, and, indeed, any 'black list' to which you refer, existed anywhere in the Corporation." The literary broadcasts to Europe would not be limited to writers who toed the government line—"any such idea would destroy the very nature of the programme"—and "nobody has so far raised any query against your name." Rilla invited Comfort to discuss "the whole matter" with him over lunch.[9]

The invitation was accepted. Following their meeting, Comfort sent Rilla notes for a talk, which Rilla proceeded to turn into a rough script for a dialogue between them. This he sent to Comfort on October 18. Comfort's final sentences could almost serve as a summation of the mission he and his fellow anarcho-pacifists had been pursuing for the past four years: "We set ourselves a task in 1940—we tried to keep sane, to remember we were human beings, not to be taken in by hate-propaganda from either side. We've tried to stick to the ideal of personal responsibility and artistic freedom. I don't think we've done too badly. At any rate, we've kept on writing."

Cryptically, Rilla wrote that he still had to get in touch with Hilton Brown, the novelist and poet who was head of talks at the BBC, to "clear up your position" before the program could go forward, noting that Brown had been hard to reach. Nevertheless, he reminded Comfort that the recording date was set for Wednesday, October 25, from 2:00 pm to 2:30 pm.[10]

On October 23, however, Comfort received a letter from the actor and writer Robert Speaight, then working for the network, informing him that his contribution to the program on "the present situation and prospects for English literature" would not be used. By way of explanation, and with utmost tact, Speaight wrote,

> You will, I think, realise that the European Service is bound by rather strict political considerations and we have to be very careful about letting anything on the air which might be liable to misinterpretation by our listeners. I wholly respect the sincerity and frankness of your views, but I do feel that they might very easily be misunderstood and lead people to think that they are more generally shared in this country than in fact I believe they are. I should not wish to constrain you to any false modification of what you evidently feel very strongly and so I hope we may allow the matter to rest where it stands with no ill will on either side.[11]

Comfort would not appear on the BBC airwaves again until four years after the war. His treatment echoes Randolph Bourne's plight after he published "War and the Intellectuals" in the *Seven Arts* during the previous world war. The article attracted so much outrage that the magazine shut down; Bourne was edged out of editorial conferences at another leading arts journal, *The Dial*, and was limited to writing book reviews for the duration of the war—one of which he headlined, appropriately, "Clipped Wings."[12]

But the BBC's awkward dance with Comfort also bespeaks the muddled politics of the war's last year, when more people were willing to criticize the slaughter but the government and much of the public were still inclined to crack down. Vera Brittain, along with signing Comfort's manifesto, published a short book, *Seed of Chaos: What*

Mass Bombing Really Means, which collected eyewitness accounts of the saturation bombing of German cities. It served to draw more attention to the issue, especially among clergy in the UK and the United States, but was attacked strongly by the mainstream press of both countries. When an abridged version was published in the United States as *Massacre by Bombing*, the editors of the *New York Times* concluded, "We should leave tactics and strategies to the generals hoping they can be as merciful as they can. . . . But let us not deceive ourselves into thinking that war can be made humane."[13] The prominent journalist William L. Shirer, later the author of *The Rise and Fall of the Third Reich*, attacked Brittain as a stooge for Nazi lies about the bombing casualties.[14]

In his May 19, 1944, "As I Please" column for *Tribune*, Orwell called Brittain's book "an eloquent attack on indiscriminate or 'obliteration' bombing," but he criticized her for seemingly accepting the need to win the war while condemning the means of doing so. "Now, no one in his senses regards bombing, or any other operation of war, with anything but disgust," he wrote. "On the other hand, no decent person cares tuppence for the opinion of posterity. And there is something very distasteful in accepting war as an instrument and at the same time wanting to dodge responsibility for its obviously barbarous features. . . . All talk of 'limiting' or 'humanizing' war is sheer humbug."

Why should armies make any distinction between combatants and noncombatants? Orwell asked.

> Obviously one must not kill children if it is in any way avoidable, but it is only in propaganda pamphlets that every bomb drops on a school or an orphanage. A bomb kills a cross-section of the population. . . . On the other hand, "normal" or "legitimate" warfare picks out and slaughters all the healthiest and bravest young

male population. Every time a German submarine goes
to the bottom about fifty young men of fine physique
and good nerves are suffocated.[15]

In a column two months later, responding to some mail he
had received about his critique, Orwell allowed that "I am
definitely tired of bombs," but he then went on to defend
indiscriminate bombing and sketch a bizarrely biological
perspective on whose lives were worth preserving in wartime. "It is probably somewhat better to kill a cross-section
of the population than to kill only the young men. . . . Had
[the last war] been conducted, as the next one probably will
be, with flying bombs, rockets or other long-range weapons which kill old and young, healthy and unhealthy, male
and female impartially, it would probably have damaged
European civilization somewhat less than it did."[16]

Not everyone dismissed Brittain's arguments in *Seed
of Chaos* as "humbug" or was willing to apply a relativistic
veneer to aerial bombing of population centers—and the
knowledge that this small but persistent opposition existed
had a least some effect on the government. We have already noted Comfort's aphorism, in *Partisan Review*, that
"Hitler's greatest and irretrievable victory . . . was when
he persuaded the English people that the only way to lick
Fascism was to imitate it." He and other pacifists repeated
this argument over and over during the war years, and it
hindered the government from making a straightforward
defense of its bombing policy for fear of offering proof to
its critics.

Attempting to explain to a private audience in late
1941 why Bomber Command couldn't tell the public that
it had been "attacking people" for well over a year, Peirse
said it was necessary for the public to believe "that we still
held some scruples and only attacked what the humani-
tarians are pleased to call military targets." When Harris,
his successor, argued for changing the policy the following

year, he was told, much to his irritation, that Air Ministry didn't want to provoke "religious and humanitarian opinions." "Liberal opinion is a bit sticky about bombing," Air Minister Sir Archibald Sinclair told Churchill in December 1942. This "stickiness," and the fear of being compared morally to the Nazis, is likely an important reason that

We only hit "vital industrial areas": British war propaganda poster, 1943. Courtesy World War Poster Collection, Upper Midwest Literary Archives, University of Minnesota Libraries

pacifists had as much latitude as they did for dissent during
the war, historian Richard Overy argues.[17]

Neither mainstream Britain nor the government was
ready to accept that the State had anything to apologize
for in its conduct of the war, as Orwell's columns and the
BBC's nudging-out of Comfort suggest. Less than two
months after Comfort last heard from the BBC, a far more
disturbing incident took place. Armed with a warrant

Turning RAF bombing into German propaganda:
"The enemy sees your light! Blackout!"
German war propaganda poster, unknown date

issued under Defence Regulation 39A, which made it an offense to "endeavour to cause disaffection amongst persons engaged . . . in his Majesty's Service," a squad from Special Branch raided the premises of Freedom Press. According to Woodcock, the raid was in response to a manifesto recently published in *War Commentary* that the editors intended to circulate to members of the armed forces, calling on them to practice mass disobedience as soon as the war was over, if not before.[18]

The warrant authorized the police only to seize evidence of such acts, but they ransacked the offices, clearing out the entire contents of letter trays, invoices and account books, even the office typewriter—in short, everything the collective needed to carry on business. Two months passed before any of the items were returned. At the same time, Special Branch raided the homes of at least five members of the collective, including Vernon Richards and Marie Louise Berneri, seizing personal correspondence, literary manuscripts, and check stubs. Shortly thereafter, soldiers and sailors who had corresponded with Freedom Press or subscribed to its publications had their kits searched; copies of *War Commentary*, *Peace News*, and *NOW* were seized.[19]

As soon as they got word of the raids, Comfort, Read, and Woodcock met and decided to petition a wide list of writers, artists, and other public personalities to sign a letter protesting this ruthless attempt to suppress dissent. With the war clearly winding toward its end, public figures were less reluctant to criticize the government, and the three obtained signatures from a wide range of luminaries, including T. S. Eliot, E. M. Forster, Dylan Thomas, Cyril Connolly, Stephen Spender, Osbert Sitwell, and Bertrand Russell.[20] Orwell signed a separate letter, along with Comfort, Thomas, and the painter Jankel Adler. In May, four members of the Freedom Press group were tried at the Old Bailey for conspiring "to undermine the affections of members of His Majesty's Forces."

The Freedom Press Defence Committee was set up with Read as chair, Orwell as vice-chair, and Woodcock as secretary. Berneri was acquitted because under English law a wife could not conspire with her husband, while the three male editors received comparatively light sentences of nine months imprisonment at Wormwood Scrubs.[21]

The publicity the case received and the support of prominent people, who by then also included Harold Laski, Augustus John, Sybil Thorndike, and Henry Moore, helped mitigate the punishments. The trial itself helped spread the very ideas the government had attempted to suppress, Woodcock remembered: "All the so-called seditious writings—poetry and prose—on which the prosecution based its case were read in court, and the daily papers reported them almost verbatim, so that ideas that had previously reached only a few thousand people through *War Commentary* now reached several millions, courtesy of Lord Beaverbrook and Lord Rothermere."[22]

Afterward, the support group was reorganized as the Freedom Defence Committee, a civil liberties watchdog, which met in the back room of the Freedom Press bookshop and typed its letters and appeals on a typewriter once owned by Orwell's late wife Eileen, which he donated.[23] Orwell continued to serve as vice-chair—the only office he ever accepted—until the committee dissolved in 1949.

This suggests how the political atmosphere had changed by the end of the war. For instance, when Comfort asked Spender to sign his declaration against civilian bombing, the poet had declined; when the Freedom Press case materialized, Spender was willing to say yes, although he dragged his feet. "Characteristically," he then kept away from civil liberties issues after being reprimanded by his boss at the Foreign Office, Woodcock recalled.[24] Orwell by this time permitted himself to go farther in print in deploring war than he had just a couple of years earlier. In an August 1944 "As I Please" column in *Tribune*, he wrote,

> War damages the fabric of civilisation, not by the de-
> struction it causes . . . not even by the slaughter of
> human beings, but by stimulating hatred and dishon-
> esty. By shooting at your enemy you are not in the
> deepest sense wronging him. But by hating him, by
> inventing lies about him and bringing children up to be-
> lieve them, by clamouring for unjust peace terms which
> make further wars inevitable, you are striking not at one
> perishable generation, but at humanity itself.[25]

The Freedom Press raid must have had an especially powerful effect on Orwell, given his experience of political
persecution in Spain. Not only did Special Branch deprive
the collective of the physical necessities of publication, but
it also had a chilling effect on its outside relationships as
well. Its landlord forbade it to carry on business on the
premises, and it had difficulty finding new offices. Its
paper supplier cut it off. Orwell helped organize a letter
from the Freedom Defence Committee in 1948 protesting
the sacking of people considered to be politically suspect
from the Civil Service and demanding a fair process for
them to defend themselves against any charges.[26]

As he came to know the Freedom collective better
through Read, Comfort, and Woodcock, Orwell became
friends with some of its other members—people he had
castigated only a couple of years before. In his December 8,
1944, "As I Please" column, he went so far as to regret his
old habit of describing pacifists as "objectively" profascist
even though they were personally hostile to fascism: "I
have been guilty of saying this myself more than once." At
one point he offered *Animal Farm* to Freedom Press after
Gollancz turned it down, but Berneri, the forceful manag-
ing editor, rejected the manuscript out of hand, allegedly
unable to forgive Orwell's attacks on anarchists during the
war, although her husband and coeditor, Vernon Richards,
later denied this.[27]

Nevertheless, Orwell accepted an invitation to address the London Anarchist Group, a weekly speaker series and discussion group, on "Trends in Russia's Foreign Policy" on January 20, 1946, although he declined an invitation to address the PPU at about the same time.[28]

Orwell, who disliked being photographed, even allowed Richards and Berneri to take a series of photos of him at home, which was published by Freedom Press decades later as *George Orwell at Home (and among the Anarchists): Essays and Photographs*. They are the last photos of him that survive. (Richards and Berneri also took numerous portraits and book-jacket photos of Comfort and Read in these years.) When the last copies of the original print run of *Homage to Catalonia* were remaindered after Orwell's death in 1950, Freedom Press acquired the lot.[29]

By this time, two of the writers Orwell had attacked in *Partisan Review* in 1942, Woodcock and Julian Symons,[30] were close friends of his, and Orwell and Comfort were friendly if not close. Orwell gave Woodcock a considerable donation from his *Animal Farm* earnings to keep *NOW* running, despite the fact that Woodcock's writings in the first issue of the magazine had helped precipitate his attack on pacifists in *Partisan Review*.[31]

This is not as paradoxical as it might seem. Whatever Orwell's objections to anarchism, anarchists themselves were an important component of the anticommunist Left with which he generally identified himself, starting in Spain, and he couldn't help but notice that their viewpoints overlapped with his. Emma Goldman headed the English section of Solidaridad Internacional Antifascista (SIA), the support group set up by the Confederación Nacional del Trabajo (CNT), Spain's anarcho-syndicalist labor federation, in 1937–1938, and she had run up against much the same hostility from the communist-leaning English Left that Orwell had.[32] When *Homage to Catalonia* appeared, Goldman wrote that she "wished it could be circulated

Vernon Richards and Marie Louise Berneri.
Photo: Archivio Berneri

in tens of thousands of copies," including in the United
States, so as to "expose the conspiracy against [the Spanish
anarchists] to the world."[33]

As for Richards and Berneri, they were, like Orwell,
strongly anti-Soviet, and their hostility had equally personal origins. Berneri's father, the Italian anarchist and
antifascist Camillo Berneri, had organized the first brigade
of Italian volunteers to fight against Franco's insurrection

in Spain. There he was murdered by members of the Communist Party. Richards, who began life as Vero Recchioni, a second-generation Italian anarchist, had come to know Orwell slightly in London in 1938 when both were supporters of the SIA. *War Commentary*, the paper Berneri and Richards ran during the war and to which Comfort was a frequent contributor, began life in 1936 as *Spain and the World*, an outlet in Britain for Goldman and other supporters of the Spanish non-Communist Left; after the fall of the republic, it changed its name to *Revolt!* for a short time—Orwell wrote Herbert Read in March 1939 that he would like to write for it[34]—before becoming *War Commentary*. After the war, Richards and Berneri retitled it *Freedom*, the name under which it continued to appear until 2014.

That some members of the Freedom Press collective could not see past Orwell's previous hostility made little difference; he was uninterested in identifying himself with any particular group or tendency. In fact, the Freedom Defence Committee was the only voluntary body, other than the ILP, the Home Guard, and the National Union of Journalists, that he ever joined.

One event in particular brought Orwell, Comfort, and the anarchists into much closer alignment: the dropping of the atomic bomb. Comfort condemned the destruction of Hiroshima and Nagasaki in an article in *War Commentary* less than three weeks after the August 6 and 9 attacks. He brought to it some of the strongest language he would ever use in print:

> We have just witnessed an act of criminal lunacy which must be without parallel in recorded history. A city of 300,000 people has been suddenly and deliberately obliterated and its inhabitants murdered by the English [*sic*] and American governments. . . . We have dissented and protested in the past, but the time for dissent

and protest are over. The men who did this are criminal
lunatics. Unless this final atrocity is irrevocably and un-
questionably brought home to them by public opinion,
we have no claim to be human beings.[35]

Comfort framed the nuclear attacks as a logical extension
of the Allied bombing campaign and more than two decades of state infatuation with aerial warfare, which, he
argued, had conditioned the public to accept atrocities as
just another element of modern war. "The sickening cant
about indiscriminate bombardment, the lies about liberty
and justice, have appeared for what they are," he wrote.
"One need only consider how last Monday's announce-
ment would have affected the nation if it had been made
in 1937 to realise how profoundly our responsibility has
degenerated, and how much the practice of fascism has
been sold to us since then. An endless iteration of enemy
brutality has been used to acclimatise us to crimes which
have now reached the magnitude of this massacre."

Orwell, writing in *Tribune* in October and with the
benefit of a couple of months' distance from the actual
events, was less focused on the Bomb's impact on mass psychology than its effect on the State itself—and this left him
gravely pessimistic. "The discovery of the atomic bomb, so
far from reversing history, will simply intensify the trends
which have been apparent for a dozen years at least," he
wrote. Chiefly, he was thinking of the rise of a very few
superpowers that he feared would dominate the world,
forging "an epoch as horribly stable as the slave empires
of antiquity." Without quite saying so, he indicated that
three empires would dominate this new "permanent state
of 'cold war,'" most likely some combination of Western
Europe and the United States, the Soviet Union, and "East
Asia, dominated to China."[36]

The Bomb, because of the industrial resources needed to produce it, would reinforce and speed up this grim

trend, which foreshadowed the dystopia he was already turning into compelling fiction in the manuscript of *Nineteen Eighty-Four*.

In what reads like an aside to his friends in the Freedom Press group, Orwell wrote, "Looking at the world as a whole, the drift for many decades has been not towards anarchy but towards the reimposition of slavery." What could stop it? Only two things: either "demographic changes" that he failed to specify or else the development of cheap and easily manufactured weapons that were "not dependent on huge concentration of industrial plant."

Comfort read Orwell's prophetic piece with great interest and shot off a letter to the *Tribune* editors in response. Acknowledging that "Orwell puts his finger, as usual, on the wider analytical point" that different types of weapons tend to produce particular types of societies, he nevertheless argued that "another conclusion is possible besides mere resignation to the omnipotence of tyrants equipped with nuclear energy. Not only are social institutions dictated by weapon-power: so are revolutionary tactics, and it seems to me that Orwell has made the case for the tactical use of disobedience, which he has tended to condemn in the past as pacifism."[37]

"Few if any new techniques have been devised or can be devised to counter disobedience," he argued. Comfort was never a pure nonviolent pacifist: He saw guerrilla resistance campaigns such as that of the Maquis as a potential route to postwar liberation, which is why he tended not to precede "disobedience" with "civil." Between the two wings of the wartime British peace movement, those who were absolutely opposed to war and those who only objected to civilian bombing, he came down somewhere in the middle. Whether it involved violence or not, however, Comfort did not see disobedience as assuming a formal military structure, instead relying on the individual's sense of moral responsibility.

As such, it ran directly against the trend favoring the creation of "a stable order of tyranny" that Orwell fore-saw[38]—and toward something approaching a directly democratic, anarchist vision of society. The very size of the State and the complexity of its new weapon systems would work against it while its opponents' smallness and agili-ty would help them—but only if they chose to withdraw support rather than compromise. "Political pacifism must move from objection, which is apolitic, to resistance," Comfort wrote in *Peace News* in December.[39]

Orwell's and Comfort's responses to the Bomb ap-peared in the context of the postwar European debate about what was to come next: Slavery or liberation? Cooperation or mass destruction? Already the previous fall, in another London Letter to *Partisan Review*, Orwell wrote that he had given up hope that a social revolution of some kind would accompany a British victory: "I over-emphasized the anti-Fascist character of the war, exaggerated the enormous strength of the social changes that were actually occurring, and underrated the enormous strength of the forces of reac-tion. This unconscious falsification coloured all my earlier letters to you, though perhaps not the more recent ones."[40]

This striking confession closely tracks the conclusions that Comfort and other war resisters had reached years before.

If Orwell had once condemned Comfort and his friends as defeatists, or even as an unwitting fifth column, Com-fort saw that Orwell was now himself sliding into a kind of defeatism. Both were right, in their particular ways: Or-well, that a global political stalemate had begun and that the Bomb and the technological arms race accompanying it would take the power and pervasiveness of the State to new levels; and Comfort, that there were ways, some of them highly effective, for rebels and dissidents to bring about so-cial and political change in the teeth of State domination.

VI. THE SOCIOPATHIC STATE

Comfort and Orwell met in person for the first and only time in 1945, just after the Freedom Press trial and the publication of *Animal Farm*—as Comfort remembered, at a pub in Bermondsey. By this time, Comfort was resident medical officer at the Royal Waterloo Hospital, and Orwell had left *Tribune*, although he was still contributing his "As I Please" columns to the paper. "I was shocked to see how ill he looked," Comfort reported in a remembrance and reassessment written almost forty years later. Its title, "1939 and 1984: George Orwell and the Vision of Judgment," referenced the Byron satire that had inspired their exchange of poems in *Tribune*.

Their conversation testifies that the war had only deepened Orwell's absorption in the matter that both he and Comfort had attacked from different angles: how individuals, and particularly writers and artists, should conduct themselves in the face of war and an all-encompassing State. Comfort, in his Hornbooke satires, had chalked up most artists' and intellectuals' wartime collaboration with the government to opportunism. Orwell, now that the end of the war had released him from the need to defend the government, was looking ahead to new forms of cooptation. He "told me about the new novel he was working on, *Nineteen Eighty-Four*, which I took to be a political statement against dictatorship," Comfort recalled. "His reply was astonishing—that it was, but that the model in his mind was also that of the neurotic's internal 'thought police,' with Big Brother as the superego."[1]

Did Comfort's writings, before and after meeting Orwell, influence the direction that Orwell's novel would take? Nothing in their correspondence or in Orwell's other published work confirms (or contradicts) this. But it is hard to read *Nineteen Eighty-Four*—which Orwell had first outlined in 1943 as "The Last Man in Europe"[2]—and the articles and essays he produced in the postwar years alongside Comfort's political writings from the same period and not be struck by the close parallels in the development of their thought.*

In reading the novel, "we need to experience the world as it was when Orwell cast his mind forward to 1984," Comfort later wrote. Now that the war with Germany had concluded, both were preoccupied with power itself—how it is exercised and the subtler ways in which it compels obedience. Orwell based much of the functioning of the Ministry of Truth on his experience at the BBC, and, in Comfort's reading, *Nineteen Eighty-Four* is an extrapolation of a nightmare scenario they had shared: what might have happened if England and Nazi Germany had made common cause against the Soviets and the two sides had destroyed each other, "leaving only the indestructible apparatchiks." "Hybridize the coerciveness and bureaucracy of Andropov's Russia with the glossiness and rhetoric of Reagan's America, and you have *Nineteen Eighty-Four*," Comfort concluded in his essay.[3]

---

*   Others in their wider circle were similarly preoccupied. During the same years, Marie Louie Berneri was writing her study of classic utopian and dystopian writings from Plato to Huxley, *Journey through Utopia*. It was published in 1950, after her death and not long after *Nineteen Eighty-Four* appeared.

"The really well-trained dog is the one that turns his somersault when there is no whip," Orwell had written during the war, and his novel is an unparalleled examination of how the modern state creates well-trained citizens. While *Nineteen Eighty-Four* is often described as a "totalitarian" vision, what he depicts is at once more familiar than Hitler's Germany or Stalin's Russia and a step beyond the structures they established.

Orwell biographer D. J. Taylor has noted that unlike previous dystopias—Huxley's *Brave New World*,

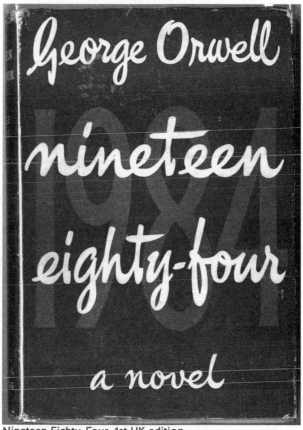

Nineteen Eighty-Four, 1st UK edition.
Courtesy Amherst College Special Collections

for example—*Nineteen Eighty-Four* takes place not in an imaginary setting but in a topography eerily close to the London that readers in the postwar years—or even in our time—would quickly recognize.[4]

The book is full of references to familiar landmarks and to the wartime experience of the Blitz. Orwell deliberately leaves the reader wondering if the world he describes is the future or, merely by inverting two digits, 1948—given, of course, the reader's ability to pierce the veil of lies and propaganda Big Brother peddles. Symons, who discussed it with him, wrote that the novel "was intended only as an extrapolation of possibilities in the nature of society inherent at the time it was written."[5]

Often in speculative fiction, the line between bleak futuristic prophecy and veiled satire of society as it exists is wafer-thin, and this is likely the case with *Nineteen Eighty-Four*. It's interesting to note, in our era of "alternative facts," that even the existence of Big Brother himself is uncertain. A statue of the leader stands in "Victory Square"—that is, Trafalgar Square—replacing Lord Nelson. His historical role is discussed extensively in *The Principles of Oligarchical Collectivism*, the book that O'Brien, an Inner Party member, gives to the unknowing Winston and which he and Julia, another would-be rebel, read and discuss in a room supplied by the shopkeeper Mr. Charrington.

But what does any of this prove? The *Principles* may be a forgery. Big Brother could be anyone—Charrington or even O'Brien, who becomes Winston's inquisitor—or no one. What proof is there, furthermore, that he is a he? Could Big Brother actually be Big Sister? Perhaps Oceania is actually controlled by a personality-less junta, or a collective leadership like the one that would succeed Stalin? Perhaps by a machine? To Orwell's characters, however, it's all the same. Enmeshed in a web of artifice and engineered truth, they are part of the composite—the "superego" that Orwell had described to Comfort at their meeting—that supports and maintains that "truth." They, and not Big Brother, are what's essential to its continuation. This was a much more sophisticated understanding of the State than Orwell had revealed in any of his previous writings, and bears some resemblance to the Marxist theorist Antonio Gramsci's views on the crucial role of culture and social relations in maintaining political control.

Comfort was thinking along similar lines. In an influential series of lectures published in 1946 as *Art and Social Responsibility*—Adrian Mitchell, the poet and antinuclear activist, said he carried a copy in his kit bag—Comfort set out the following situation, which could almost have described the social predicament, and the solution to it, that Orwell was devising for Winston Smith at about the same time:

> The man whom one knows—a good fellow, able to live as an individual a life which is free from any conscious assaults on the right of others, who does not make a practice of beating his own head or the heads of others against the walls, who is sane, with whom one eats and drinks . . . this same man can very well return one evening to talk or drink with you again and catalogue the most grotesque and contemptible actions which he has performed, or which he supports, with full approval and a fixed delusional sense of their rightness, solely because he is now acting as a member of some organised and irresponsible group. He will pay any price to rid himself of the selfhood which, subconsciously, he knows must die.[6]

But Orwell faced another problem in creating *Nineteen Eighty-Four*: If he was going to emphasize the effects of a modern authoritarian regime on its subjects and their complicity in it, where would he find room to examine the structure of the regime itself? Systems like the one he depicted depend on the availability of willing participants, but they still need people to manage and direct them. Who were these people and how did they get that way?

Paul Flewers, a scholar of the Russian Revolution and the early Soviet decades, points out that the flaw in *Animal Farm* is the author's failure to explain why the pigs become the ruling elite on the farm, or indeed why a ruling elite of any kind has to form—this development is simply a given.[7] Orwell, impatient as always with political theory, failed to fill in the ideology behind the animals' revolt except in very broad strokes, so it is not clear whether the tyranny that followed was programmed into the upheaval from the start or was instead a wrong turn on a path that started out positively. The book was "intended to show what can happen when power-hungry people" take charge of a popular struggle and that "you can't have a revolution unless you make it for yourself," Orwell wrote to Dwight Macdonald.[8]

Yet, because he did not explain how or why the animal elite selected itself, he made it easy for the Right to embrace the book, taking it as a demonstration that any leftist revolution—or, perhaps, any leftist electoral victory—was bound to end in a Stalinoid tyranny. Likewise, *Nineteen Eighty-Four* has very little to say about how the elites of the three superstates came into being, other than simple lust for power. Nor does it allow us inside the deliberative process of these elites to see the dynamic that produced their decisions.[*]

Comfort offered a partial answer less than a year after *Nineteen Eighty-Four* appeared—and shortly after Orwell's death—in a treatise titled *Authority and Delinquency in the Modern State: A Criminological Approach to the Problem of Power*. The book takes off from Comfort's assertion in his wartime writings that the individuals in positions of leadership who had ordered the invasion of other countries, the bombing of civilians, the building of

[*]   See O'Brien's explanation to Winston Smith in George Orwell, *Nineteen Eighty-Four* (London: Harmondsworth, 1969), 211–12.

the death-camp system, and finally the creation and use of the atomic bomb were criminal psychopaths. The nature of the modern State is to select such people for positions of power and then to encourage their "delinquent" behavior.[9]

In his introduction to a slightly revised edition of the book twenty years later, Comfort wrote of "the growing awareness that, great as is the nuisance-value of the criminal in urban society, the centralized pattern of government

AUTHORITY
and
DELINQUENCY
in the
MODERN STATE

A Criminological Approach

to the Problem of Power

by

ALEX COMFORT

Authority and Delinquency in the Modern State,
1st UK edition. Courtesy Nicholas Comfort

is to-day dependent for its continued function upon a supply of individuals whose personalities and attitudes in no way differ from those of admitted psychopathic delinquents. . . . The egocentric psychopath who swindles in the financial field is punishable—if his activities are political, he enjoys immunity and esteem, and may take part in the determination of laws."[10]

The British historian Lord Acton famously stated that "absolute power corrupts absolutely," and the Russian anarchist Mikhail Bakunin came to a similar conclusion. "Nothing is more dangerous for man's private morality than the habit of command," he wrote. "The best man, the most intelligent, disinterested, generous, pure, will infallibly and always be spoiled at this trade."[11]

Comfort went further, arguing that the State deliberately molds and recruits "delinquents" for positions of power.

What makes a person a "delinquent"? "The chief factor," Comfort argued, "is the assertion . . . of the right of the actor to behave without regard of others. . . . The opportunities for this kind of accepted and acceptable delinquency lie almost entirely within the pattern of power."[12]

In the United States, the Authorization for Use of Military Force (AUMF) that followed the September 11, 2001, terrorist attacks translated this "assertion" into law, giving the Bush administration the authority to take whatever actions it deemed necessary against the people who "planned, authorized, committed or aided" the attackers and against individuals who harbored them. Since then, presidents have used the AUMF as protective cover for a far wider assortment of military actions; later versions of the bill have enabled further undeclared American wars in Iraq (2002) and Syria (2013), and an amendment by Senator Rand Paul to force a vote on a new authorization was soundly defeated in September 2017.

The growing size, reach, and complexity of the State make it more rather than less likely to attract people with a "delinquent" frame of mind—and to place the vast powers of the AUMF in their hands. Comfort wrote: "The centralized system of election . . . selects very heavily against the principled and the moderate, and against those leadership-attributes which depend on face-to-face contacts. The rational leader may ultimately have a decreasing chance against the determined climber and the psychopath who reflects the attitude of the frustrated crowd, or who is living down his own failures of adjustment."[13]

Nor are strong convictions or idealism a safeguard. "Few leaders have surpassed Adolf Hitler in their sense of mission," Comfort observed. Governments in the modern era have become more rather than less preoccupied with foreign policy and war, he argued, because they give the sorts of people who occupy positions of power the biggest arena in which to posture and self-dramatize: "The insistence of such leaders on the possession of nuclear weapons is an integral part of the use to which they put the opportunities of foreign policy—they make their exits and entrances more sensational, they heighten the dramatic tension of the performance—like the street urchin's knife, they carry a pleasing ability to frighten the owner and everyone else."[14]

The difference between the "urchin" and the nuclear-enabled world leader is the State itself: molded, to some extent, by "delinquent" personalities, it encourages them to seek positions of leadership in turn by providing them with a platform from which to act out their fantasies and aggressions. The society they create emphasizes punishment and retribution over education as a way to modify behavior among the masses, encourages aggression over cooperation, pathologizes the working class when it resists its treatment under the capitalist system (as evidence, Comfort notes "suggestions that the working classes strike more often than the professional because of the more brutal parental discipline in their homes"),[15] and discourages the development of sociability as a counterweight or alternative to the

State and capitalism (encapsulated in Margaret Thatcher's later assertion, "There is no such thing as society. There are individual men and women, and there are families").[16]

All of this applies just as well to the Marxist conception of revolution, Comfort added, with "its failure to come to terms with psychopathology of office, which has distorted its constructive intentions exactly as in other societies, if not more so. . . . No real revolution can be brought about through the interplay of aggressions and projections which makes up almost the whole of traditional political thought, both governmental and revolutionary."[17]

Other writers, considering the behavior of the wartime leaders, have come to similar conclusions. In his essay "Air War and Literature," W. G. Sebald suggested that "Bomber" Harris "liked destruction for its own sake" and that his position as head of Bomber Command, not to mention his influence over Churchill's War Cabinet, "was unassailable *because* of his unlimited interest in destruction." Elias Canetti, Sebald notes, "linked the fascination of power in its purest form to the growing number of its accumulated victims."[18]

Comfort's analysis of the psychological basis of delinquency and aggression among political leaders was also a primary influence on a leading figure in social psychology, one of the disciplines he felt would be crucial to the development of an anarchist critique of the State. Stanley Milgram cited *Authority and Delinquency in the Modern State* as one of three primary influences on his research, including his famous 1960-1963 experiment in obedience, in which he tested volunteers' willingness to inflict pain on other individuals when an authority figure asked them to do so.*

Like *Authority and Delinquency*, *Nineteen Eighty-Four* was written in the immediate post-Hitler years and

---

*   Other influences on Milgram's experiment were *The Ghost in the Machine* by Orwell's friend Arthur Koestler and a conceptual analysis of authority by Robert Bierstedt. Stanley Milgram, *Obedience to Authority: An Experimental View* (New York: Harper Perennial, 1975), xv.

while Stalin was still in power, and the two tyrants cast a long shadow over the portrayal of authoritarian leaders in both books. But, as Comfort later pointed out, "Americans read *Nineteen Eighty-Four* as a nightmare based on Stalinism. To some extent it is; but Orwell's novel of Soviet Communism is *Animal Farm*."[19]

The global framework of Orwell's dystopia was the three-way, permanent war between Oceania, Eurasia, and Eastasia—a satirical recasting of the Cold War. He did not even hint at which of the three was the "right" side; the mere fact that he imagined three rather than two suggests that there is nothing much to choose between them. The constant reshuffling of alliances—one day, Eurasia is the great enemy, the next day the enemy has "always" been Eastasia—resembles in some respects the shifting configuration of U.S. policy in the Middle East, where for decades Iraq and Iran have traded places as the great enemy and first Shiites and then radical Sunnis are the sectarian foe.

There are differences between Orwell's perspective in *Nineteen Eighty-Four* and Comfort's in *Authority and Delinquency*. The State, in Comfort's portrayal, is driven directly by brutish, "barbarous" impulses, with very little subtlety overlaid. Orwell's Inner Party, in the person of O'Brien, Winston Smith's inquisitor, can be subtle, sophisticated, even intellectual in its approach. But there is very little difference at the core. "The object of persecution," Orwell has O'Brien tell Winston, "is persecution. The object of torture is torture. The object of power is power." Comfort's "delinquents" would certainly have agreed.

Comfort and Orwell both took pains not to structure their critiques around the manipulations of a single super-villain. Orwell's Big Brother is a shadowy figure, despite the cult of personality constructed around him. Comfort stressed that the characteristics of psychopaths-in-power are not unusual; every day we encounter people who could be just as abusive and murderous given the right circumstances. Comfort's treatise complements Orwell's dystopia in two ways: by attempting to create a psychological profile of Big Brother—whether he be one or many—and by advancing some ideas about how we can escape the web the modern State weaves around us.

Comfort's recipe for ending the regime of delinquents in authority, with their warlike impulses, reflected a deep faith in the power of education and scientific truth to create a more rational society. It had six ingredients:

1. Education, to promote public awareness of specific problems like war and social neuroses (in other words, to spread Comfort's own ideas).
2. Experiments in communal living and control of resources, to instill a daily practice of living and functioning outside the State.
3. Pressure (exactly what kind he did not specify) to break up larger components of government and business and to increase workers' control of production.
4. "Propaganda" and "instruction"—of both children and adults—to make sociability a more prominent part of character formation.
5. Psychiatry, which can help to "adjust" the individual in the direction of rejecting and resisting "bad institutions."
6. Public resistance and the willingness to disobey.[20]

The last was the most radical in its details, aligning with much of what Comfort had said during the war: disobedience "may involve specifically revolutionary activity, such as the encouragement of direct resistance to delinquent authority and the withdrawal of scientific support from projects involving secrecy, the suppression of information, and the abuse of technology for war purposes."[21]

Until Comfort's time, most anarchists, like the Marxists, had emphasized the economic roots of capitalism and the State and the need for the working class to unite against them. While he never denied the importance of either, Comfort expected fundamental change to come from a different direction. Believing that new trends in sociology, social anthropology, and psychology implicitly critiqued the State and capitalism and encouraged the kind of decentralized, self-managed, peaceful society he favored, Comfort argued that anarchists needed to understand and practice these disciplines and spread their insights to the public if they wanted to again build a mass movement.

This was a more effective approach to changing society in "an age of discouraged revolutionaries," he wrote, since the violent revolutions of the nineteenth and early twentieth centuries had mostly resulted not in greater freedom but in a stronger, more repressive state. Orwell came to the same conclusion in answering some critics of *Animal Farm* who had accused him of rejecting revolution: "*That kind* of revolution (violent conspiratorial revolution, led by consciously power-hungry people) can only lead to a change of masters."[22]

Against this path to change, Comfort said, in a lecture to the Anarchist Summer School in London in 1950, "I want to see something done which has not been done before—a concerted, unbiased, and properly documented attempt to disseminate accurate teaching of the result of modern child psychiatry, social psychology and political psychology to the general public on the same scale as we have in the past tried to disseminate revolutionary propaganda."[23]

Comfort's proposals were rooted in a belief, shared by others on the left, not only that human nature could be improved, but that such improvement was now necessary to keep the human race from destroying itself. The traditional governing-class view, going back to the origins of the modern State in the Renaissance and encompassing all its manifestations from liberal democracy to dictatorship to people's republic, was exactly the opposite: that no matter what age we live in, human nature is always the same, responding to the same impulses in the same way. In his intellectual biography of Machiavelli, Sebastian de Grazia writes, "The world of human things is like the deck of cards Niccolò and his pals play with up at the tavern, reshuffled and redealt, but the same cards." The State was not just a device for keeping the people in line—it was their fulfillment, their only means of achieving a society that could secure the common good. "Ineluctably, mutual impulse moves through couples, families, households, and villages to the culmination of the political animal in the state."[24]

This happy pattern of evolution was no longer obviously the best or only one in the age of mechanized, depersonalized mass death that aerial warfare was helping to bring into being, nor was it inevitable to people who rejected the notion that human nature itself was static. Preventing the end of the human race required "the moral regeneration of mankind," Herbert Read wrote; this "can be accomplished only by moral education, and until moral education is given priority over all other forms of education, I see no hope for the world."[25]

In a highly influential book, *Education through Art* (1943), Read argued for the centrality of art to education as a means of developing children's capacity for perception, self-expression, and sociability: "One of the most certain lessons of modern psychology and of recent historical experiences, is that education must be a process, not only of individuation, but also of integration, which is the reconciliation of individual uniqueness and social unity. . . . The individual will be 'good' in the degree that his individuality is realized within the organic wholeness of the community."[26]

Machiavelli and those who followed him saw the human race's only path to improvement passing through the State; Read and Comfort wanted to put the individual back at the center of human development and believed it was possible to do so. Education based on creativity was crucial because only this could nurture individuals capable of forming healthy communities on their own, without centralized institutions directing them. And education must not end with childhood. Comfort's proposals for implementing the program he laid out in 1950 included a syllabus for an anarchist encyclopedia ("a book of the

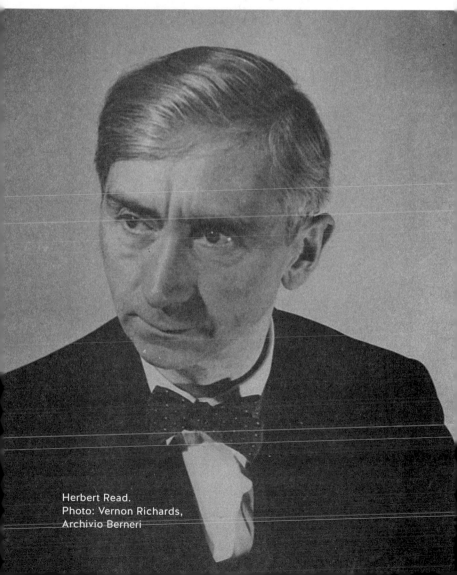

Herbert Read.
Photo: Vernon Richards,
Archivio Berneri

general stature of *Das Kapital*") that incorporated practical matters like town planning, psychology, and education; communal living experiments; and a "small anarchist exhibition" at the Festival of Britain, a program of local and touring exhibitions that the Labour government staged in 1951 to celebrate the nation's recovery from the war.

"What an optimist you are!" Read wrote in a letter to his friend, and it is difficult not to be incredulous at the notion that disseminating psychological and sociological research to the masses could summon a new cooperative society into being.[27] Neither the encyclopedia nor the anarchist exhibition came to be. Like Orwell, Comfort shied away from the fine points of political theory, although he sometimes described himself as a political theorist, and he said little about the nuts and bolts of how psychopaths govern. At times, his focus on psychology and sociology seems like an attempt to sidestep this issue.

But Comfort's idea that class struggle was not the only road to social transformation and that getting there would require a multipronged approach that included both prefigurative communities—as they would later be called—and efforts to bring about a change in human character through psychological and sociological practice grew directly from his wartime conviction that "the war is not between classes. The war is at root between individuals and barbarian society."[28]

Orwell seemed to echo this formulation a few years later in a letter to a friend: "The real division is not between conservatives and revolutionaries but between authoritarians and libertarians." Revolution and class struggle would not get very far—they could lead instead to a scenario like *Animal Farm*—unless human beings themselves first began cultivating greater sociability and fashioning a new way to live with each other.[29]

Orwell was attracted by the prospect of a new kind of politics—the kind he thought he had glimpsed in Barcelona in 1937—but he seldom attempted to envision what it might look like. In Comfort's writings, the road map becomes more distinct and more hopeful. Comfort's viewpoint would contribute to the "new anarchism" that arose after the war and, directly or indirectly, many of the popular struggles and social movements of the 1960s and beyond.

These movements shared a premise that the individual and society could reinforce each other rather than canceling each other out. The American anarchist and social ecologist Murray Bookchin, for example, was captivated by Read's idea that when the individual is placed at the center of human development, "an ever-enlarging unity is achieved by growing differentiation. An expanding whole is created by the diversification and enrichment of the parts."[30]

Building on that, Comfort began to develop an argument that connects his anarchist and pacifist writings of the 1940s with his later writings on sex: ending racism, sexism, economic exploitation, war, and other scourges of existing society was closely connected with cultural and interpersonal struggles against repressive sexual practices, gender, and family patterns, while experiments in communal living were not just self-indulgent exercises but serious attempts to prefigure new and more sustainable social patterns. Because healthy, unanxious, mutually satisfactory sex play is fundamental to the development of sociability, Comfort said, overcoming ingrained social barriers to sexual freedom was also necessary to overcome the "aggressions and projections" that perpetuate the "psychopathology of office."[31]

VII. THE "SNITCH LIST"

"You can't have a revolution unless you make it for yourself," Orwell wrote, and this idea could stand as fundamental to his brand of libertarian socialism. It also dovetails with the argument Comfort had been making both during and after the war that the only way to eliminate the ills of a "barbarian" society was for responsible individuals to refuse to cooperate with it. Among many other things, *Nineteen Eighty-Four* lays out in detail the lengths to which a totalitarian state could go to prevent its subjects from understanding themselves this way. Not surprisingly, Comfort believed that he and Orwell were growing closer in their thinking as the postwar period progressed.

"I counted Orwell as a friend," he wrote in 1983, and Comfort's son recalls that his father always spoke of Orwell with great respect.[1]

But the two men's emotional responses to the war were very different. Orwell had hoped that the English people's experience pulling together and finding a common purpose in the fight against fascism would lead to a great transformation, perhaps to the socialist society he envisioned. He "rather liked the war, for he saw it as a fight against the governing class as well as a fight against the Nazis," V. S. Pritchett remembered.[2]

When this transformation did not happen, he was deeply disappointed. Comfort, by contrast, had never expected anything of the sort, unless it began with widespread resistance to the State. After the war, then, he continued to stress the need for principled disobedience, incorporating it into the analysis he developed in *Authority and Delinquency*.

Orwell continued to pour his disappointment into the unrelenting gloom of *Nineteen Eighty-Four*. Yet he remained as concerned as ever about the threat of Stalinism; in his postwar journalism, he followed closely the swallowing up of one after another East European country by the Soviets. He also remembered well his treatment by British leftists sympathetic to Moscow; it rankled further that some people he suspected of being Russian apologists and, perhaps, covert agents had managed to rise in the BBC and the intelligence services, protected by their public-school and university connections. So concerned was he by what seemed the steady extension of Stalin's influence, both on the Continent and among influential parties at home, that in a letter to his onetime publisher Victor Gollancz, he said that if the Cold War became a shooting war between the United States and Russia, he would support the United States.[3]

Orwell kept up his friendship with many of the individuals grouped around Freedom Press. While he was being treated in a sanatorium in Gloucestershire in the spring of 1949, his adopted son Richard was put up at Whiteway Colony, a fifty-year-old Tolstoyan/anarchist community located nearby. But despite these connections, he maintained his suspicions of anarchists and pacifists. Around the same time he was meeting Comfort, he was still able to write, in a 1945 essay, "There is a minority of intellectual pacifists, whose real though unacknowledged motive appears to be hatred of western democracy and admiration of totalitarianism."[4]

Orwell, Comfort might have said, was again "intellectual-hunting." He did not specify who the members of this "minority" were, but in a letter to Arthur Koestler two years later, he suggested where the "totalitarianism" came in.

In the course of soliciting Koestler for a contribution to the Freedom Defence Committee, Orwell cautioned, "I think there may be a row about the larger aims of the Committee, because at present the moving spirits in it are anarchists and there is a tendency to use it for anarchist propaganda."[5]

Utopians, as he took anarchists to be, were in some ways more dangerous than right-wing prohibitionists, he observed, since a philosophy based on love rather than prohibition was more likely to insist on conformity: "When human beings are governed by 'thou shalt not,' the individual can practice a certain amount of eccentricity: when they are supposedly governed by 'love' or 'reason,' he is under continuous pressure to make him behave and think exactly the same as everyone else."[6]

One cannot help but remember that the State's frequently enunciated objective in *Nineteen Eighty-Four* was to get Winston Smith to "love Big Brother." But there is actually less to Orwell's equation between antiauthoritarian anarchists and authoritarian fascists—widely held to be one of his more penetrating political insights—than meets the eye because there is nothing unique about anarchism in this respect.

Certainly, an anarchist society built on consensus decision-making in a community of socioeconomic equals can take on many of the characteristics of a tyranny, given the right circumstances. But a social democracy or a liberal democracy founded on majority rule can be susceptible to the same sort of conformist pressures that Orwell described and is at least as likely to devolve into a tyranny. Americans have become familiar with this through the War on Terror, as domestic as well as foreign surveillance, indefinite detention, and torture—acts that once would have been associated with fascism—are finding passive acceptance. It is hard to imagine any open political system that couldn't slide into fascism, depending on the context and degree of cultural resistance. Hitler came to power, after all, in a country with a democratic political structure founded on a very liberal constitution—and his regime was most definitely governed by "thou shalt not."

Nevertheless, at some point in the postwar years, Orwell began keeping a notebook listing people he suspected of being either Communists or morally squishy when it came to totalitarianism. Some were writers, artists, and celebrities not personally known to him; some were people he knew and didn't like; others were people he knew and liked but didn't trust. In May 1949, just months after applying the final touches to *Nineteen Eighty-Four*, Orwell sent a cut-down list of thirty-eight names to Celia Kirwan, a friend who had taken a job with the Information Research Department (IRD) of the Foreign Office.[7] Kirwan had asked him for the list in order to warn British diplomats at the United Nations, who were approaching writers and artists to help them counter Soviet propaganda, against individuals deemed unreliable.[8]

One of these was Alex Comfort. About his friend's alleged collaborationism, Orwell wrote, "Potential only." Here is the rest of the entry, quoted earlier: "Is pacifist-anarchist. Main emphasis anti-British. Subjectively pro-German during war, appears temperamentally pro-totalitarian. Not morally courageous. Has a crippled hand. Very talented."[9]

What did this somewhat cryptic entry mean? "Potential only" clearly meant that Comfort was only "potentially" pro-Soviet; the rest we can unpack based on opinions Orwell had expressed during the previous decade. Comfort was "not morally courageous" because he had never explicitly denounced the Soviet regime—"*the* test of intellectual honesty," as Orwell put it. "Pro-German" and "anti-British" fit with Orwell's conviction that anyone who did not wholeheartedly embrace the war effort was effectively on the side of the enemy. By adding the word "subjectively," Orwell went further, implying that Comfort wasn't just a patsy of the Germans, but actively on their side—this despite the fact, again, that Comfort never wrote a sympathetic word about Hitler's regime. "Appears temperamentally pro-totalitarian" alluded to Comfort's anarchism and Orwell's argument that anarchism tends in the direction of conformist tyranny.

The Foreign Office released documents in 1996 verifying that the list existed—although Bernard Crick's biography had already mentioned it in 1980—and a truncated version appeared in Peter Davison's twenty-volume *Complete Works of George Orwell* in 1998. Davison, who had written back and forth with Comfort about some details of his correspondence with Orwell, left Comfort's name out, along with the names of seven other individuals he couldn't trace or who were still alive at the time. By then, Comfort had suffered a massive stroke and was living in a nursing home, where he was less able to keep up with current events and communicate about them. His son believes he never knew Orwell had included him on the list, a full copy of which only surfaced in 2003, three years after Comfort's death.[10]

Had he known, it's safe to say Comfort would have been taken aback. The assertions Orwell made were not very different from the accusations he had hurled at Comfort and other anarcho-pacifists during the war. But now he was making them in a letter directed to the IRD, a cog in Britain's Cold War propaganda apparatus. Objectively—to use Orwell's word—Comfort was not anti-British, pro-German, pro-Soviet, or pro-totalitarian, whatever tendencies Orwell thought he detected in his friend's actual positions. Neither was he a "crypto-Communist" or "fellow-traveller"—the words Orwell used to describe the people on his list in a letter to his friend Richard Rees.[11]

Comfort, in his wartime writings, had never offered support to either the Soviet regime or Marxist-Leninism in general. Neither had Comfort ever expressed hostility to Britain or its people, only to the British state and its government. Orwell seems to have forgotten, additionally, that in Spain in the latter stages of the Civil War, the anarchists were subjected just as much to Communist persecution and violence as the quasi-Trotskyist POUM to which he had attached himself.

In fact, Comfort had himself been the victim of pro-Soviet leanings in the British cultural world early in the war—although Orwell probably did not know it. The premiere production of his anticapitalist dystopian play, *Cities of the Plain*, by the radical Unity Theatre, was canceled in August 1941, soon after the German invasion of the Soviet Union, out of sensitivity to the fact that "the collaboration between our govt and the S.U. has become closer"—this despite the government having briefly shut down the Unity Theatre at the beginning of the war. The company had ties to the Communist Party and the Left Book Club Theatre Guild, and so long as Russia was threatened by the Nazis, it informed Comfort, "the same collaboration between classes for a specific purpose is necessary within this country." Indeed, "our own capitalists . . . are fulfilling an objectively progressive role." Under the circumstances, the company couldn't produce a play whose message was "not Open up the Western Front, but Come back from the front and deal with your own capitalists."[12]

Whatever he knew or thought he knew about some of the people on his list, Orwell seems to have been oblivious—or merely chose to ignore the fact—that sharing his personal observations with a state intelligence service was quite different from attacking or sparring with his intellectual opponents in the pages of *Tribune*. What is most striking about the list as a text is how far it departs from the practice of a writer so often praised for the analytic precision of his prose and his intense concern about the misuse of language for political purposes.

The notebook began as a kind of "parlour game" between Orwell and Rees in which they attempted to guess which public figures were most likely to sell out in the event of an invasion or dictatorship.[13] When he boiled it down and made it available to people in authority, however, it still exhibited a flippant tone and little regard for the need to separate fact from impression. Next to some of the names, in the column where he noted grounds for suspecting them of being pro-Soviet, he merely indicated "?" or "??" Why, if he had nothing substantial to say about these individuals, did he include them at all?

He had qualms; before sending it to Kirwan, he noted in a letter, "Even as it stands I imagine that this list is very libellous, or slanderous, or whatever the term is, so will you please see that it is returned to me without fail." In a letter to another friend at about the same time, he discussed the difficulty of deciding who was truly "unreliable"—that is, who was sufficiently pro-Soviet that they might, for instance, hand over military secrets to Russian intelligence under the right circumstances. "The whole difficulty is to decide where each person stands, & one has to treat each case individually."[14]

Presumably, Orwell trusted Kirwan's colleagues at the IRD to do so. One of its chief outside advisers was his friend and Kirwan's brother-in-law, Arthur Koestler; another friend, Malcolm Muggeridge, had close ties with the department; and it had subsidized Chinese, Burmese, and Arabic editions of *Animal Farm*.

Comparing the names in the notebook to those on the IRD list, however, it's clear Orwell was trying to be careful. The notebook included figures such as Paul Robeson, Katherine Hepburn, Orson Welles, Upton Sinclair, and Charlie Chaplin—people whose political views were widely known and who did not form any kind of McCarthyesque fifth column. The shorter list for the IRD was still a motley collection, probably not very useful from a spy catcher's point of view, ranging from Chaplin to Comfort's friend Nicholas Moore; from J.B. Priestley and the historian E.H. Carr to Isaac Deutscher, the ex–Communist Party member and biographer of Stalin and Trotsky ("changed views chiefly because of Jewish issue. Could change again"). "A glance through the contents pages of *Labour Monthly* and other Stalinist publications could well have provided a better list of fellow-travelers," Orwell scholar Paul Flewers concluded.[15]

But the IRD list also included Peter Smollett, head of the Soviet section at the Ministry of Information during the war and later revealed as a Soviet agent recruited by Kim Philby, and Tom Driberg, a sympathetic Labour MP later recruited by the KGB.*

All of these people were either publicly prominent or occupied sensitive positions and had, at one time or another, expressed sympathy with the Soviet Union, however limited—all, that is, except Alex Comfort. While he was known in intellectual circles for his poetry, fiction, and political writings, Comfort was by no means a celebrity, and his day job was not politically sensitive. He was also the only anarchist to appear on the IRD list, although Orwell included a notation "? Anarchist leanings" next to Moore—who actually identified as a Marxist in a general sense.[16] Others whom Orwell knew well, such as George

---

* Smollett may have lobbied with Gollancz to keep *Animal Farm* from being published, although Orwell probably did not know this. Timothy Garton Ash, "Orwell's List," *New York Review of Books*, September 25, 2003.

Woodcock and his longtime friend Herbert Read, do not appear, even though Read, in particular, was a frequent guest on the BBC.

Why, then, was Comfort included while Read and Woodcock were not? For one thing, Woodcock and Read were closer friends with Orwell than Comfort ever was. And, unlike them, Comfort stepped up his political agitation after the war ended. At the same time that he was dissecting the pathology of power in *Authority and Delinquency*, he continued to call upon artists and writers, in *Art and Social Responsibility*, to embrace disobedience to a "barbarian" society directed by delinquents in positions of leadership. As Orwell grew more concerned about the possibility that fellow travelers could undermine Western resolve in the struggle against Soviet communism, he again perceived Comfort, despite their friendship, as he had during the war: as a witless apologist and a threat to national morale.

When the existence of Orwell's list became known, and later when the notebook list was partially revealed in the *Complete Works*, many expressed shock and anger. Journalist Alexander Cockburn, whose father, Claud, had run afoul of Orwell during the Spanish Civil War for publishing reports in the UK *Daily Worker* that followed the Communist Party line, labeled the notebook a "snitch list."[17] The historian John Newsinger called it "a terrible mistake on [Orwell's] part, deriving in equal measure from his hostility to Stalinism and his illusions in the Labour government."[18]

When the entire list was published in 2003, the writer and academic Norman Ian Mackenzie, who was on Orwell's list and who later worked with Comfort in the Campaign for Nuclear Disarmament, saw it as the dying writer's misguided gesture at settling scores. "Tubercular people often could get very strange towards the end," Mackenzie told the *Guardian*. "I'm an Orwell man, I agreed with him on the Soviet Union, but he went partly ga-ga I think. He let his dislike of the *New Statesman* crowd, of what he saw as leftish, dilettante, sentimental socialists who covered up for the Popular Front in Spain get the better of him."[19]

Quickly, however, a more apologetic view took hold. Already in 1996, Bernard Crick concluded, "He did it because he thought the Communist Party was a totalitarian menace. He wasn't denouncing these people as subversives. He was denouncing them as unsuitable for a counter-intelligence operation."[20]

Christopher Hitchens echoed Crick's view in his 2002 book, *Why Orwell Matters*, noting that some of the people Orwell included in the list were indeed dubious characters and even arguing that the IRD effort to recruit democratic-socialist intellectuals, rather than ostracizing them, was "part of the reason why there was no McCarthyite purge in Britain."[21]

When the shortened notebook list appeared two years later, Celia Kirwan herself took more or less the same line: "I think George was quite right to do it. . . . And, of course, everybody thinks that these people were going to be shot at dawn. The only thing that was going to happen to them was that they wouldn't be asked to write for the Information Research Department."[22]

The first in-depth piece on the list, by the Cold War historian Timothy Garton Ash, appeared in the *New York Review of Books* in 2003, soon after the list was published in full and with the cooperation of Kirwan's daughter. There is no direct evidence that any of the people on the list, including Driberg and Smollett, saw their careers curtailed as a result, Garton Ash noted; it is more than possible that the IRD did nothing with it aside from not asking the enumerated individuals to write anything. Comfort was once again a guest on the BBC in 1949, and the network continued to host him frequently on both radio and TV for decades.

If this was a witch hunt, Garton Ash concluded, "one is struck by how mild it was compared with the American

McCarthyism, which prompted Arthur Miller to write *The Crucible* and Charlie Chaplin to flee back to Orwell's Britain. . . . If the charge is that Orwell was a secret police informer, the answer is plainly no."

But the matter is not so simple because the IRD itself was not as innocuous an organization as some supposed. Its budget was voted in secret, and its purpose, according to one former employee, "was to produce and distribute and circulate unattributable propaganda."[23]

The department compiled "factual" reports and briefs that it then passed on to sympathetic members of the British intelligentsia to recycle in their own writings. Knowing who was reliable and unreliable for this work was valuable information that the intelligence services would certainly have wanted to possess as well. Adam Watson, the IRD's second-in-command, later told historian Frances Stonor Saunders that while the "immediate usefulness [of Orwell's list] was that these were not people who should write for us, [their] connections with Soviet-backed organizations *might have to be exposed at some later date.*"[24]

The IRD's mission later evolved in more dubious directions. "By the late 1950s," Garton Ash wrote, "according to someone who worked for British intelligence agencies at that time, IRD had a reputation as 'the dirty tricks department' of the Foreign Office, indulging in character assassination, false telegrams, putting itching powder on lavatory seats, and other such cold war pranks."[25]

That no one on Orwell's list came in for such treatment was, perhaps, not so much because the IRD was scrupulous in its use of information but because of his careless tone, which may have undermined the list's credibility with Foreign Office higher-ups.

Though Orwell's submission to the IRD was not a blacklist—he wasn't seeking to get anyone fired from their job—it brought Comfort and dozens of other individuals to the attention of a state intelligence apparatus that might abuse that information. And while many of these individuals were already strongly identified as leftists, being tagged as unreliable by another prominent writer of the Left could only have put them at greater risk, given the atmosphere of the time. That in the end his intervention didn't affect their careers doesn't make it all right, and Orwell, given his experience in Spain and, later, his involvement in the Freedom Press case, should have understood the dangers to which he was exposing people whose motives and actions he himself wasn't clear about in many cases. His apparent obliviousness to this is even more striking given that he assembled his list during the same years that the House Un-American Activities Committee, in the United States, was conducting its postwar witch hunts—a development that the well-informed Orwell certainly knew about.

That he was the author of *Nineteen Eighty-Four* only makes this more puzzling. Much of the substance of his novel concerned Winston Smith's growing determination not to take part in the fabrication of official history by the state—a history he knew to be full of lies and omissions but was literally the only history Big Brother would allow anyone to entertain. Orwell's letters and other writings make it clear that he knew he had been engaged in something similar during his years at the BBC. Comfort's determination to expose the government's behavior during its air war against Germany—to haul the government before the court of public opinion while it was still engaged in the war, not afterward—was not dissimilar from Winston Smith's impulse, especially keeping in mind that Oceania, too, had the excuse of being at war.

Once again, and whether he understood himself to be doing so or not, Orwell was helping the state create an official narrative, this time of the UK's tug-of-war with the Soviet Union, by urging that certain individuals—those he felt might complicate the message in ways that cast Britain and America in a bad light—not be asked to write for the IRD. This narrative would not include Chaplin, and so would exclude the American Red-baiting of the post-war years. Another name on the list was the Trinidadian Pan-Africanist George Padmore, eliminating at least one important voice of the growing anti-imperial consciousness in Britain's colonial possessions. "Reliably pro-Russian," Orwell noted, although Padmore had broken with the Communist Party in 1934 over Stalin's abuses. "Main emphasis anti-white," Orwell added, although if this were true, Padmore probably had some good reasons for feeling so.

By including Comfort in his list, Orwell was urging the IRD to exclude an individual with whose political philosophy he disagreed and who, he feared, would have muddled the anti-Soviet narrative by bringing up his own government's failures of humanity. Certainly, dissidents had other outlets for their views, but by counseling the IRD not to have dealings with them, Orwell was participating in an effort to craft an early, sanitized narrative of the Western side of the Cold War for the global public.

Numerous explanations have been offered as to why he gave the list to the IRD, including his failing health—which didn't stop him from completing his most ambitious novel—and an old infatuation with Kirwan. Certainly, his anger at the British Left was an ingredient. Years later, and in another connection, Comfort detected something else: a certain naïveté and a certain overconfidence in English political culture. Focusing on institutional Britain's response to the rise of fascism, and just how reactionary the nation's leadership might in fact have been, he wrote,

> [Orwell] had no love of these institutions, judged by their performance, but he was as profoundly English as Churchill, and Englishness imposes rules even on revolution. . . . He would have been the last person to agree that politics were governed by the rules of cricket, but the unconscious assumption remained that the "bosses,"

the opposition, though they might commit barbarities, weren't cannibals. If that were not so, if there were no limits to what Tory Britain would do to defeat change, then we were headed for political Gehenna.[26]

While Comfort had little difficulty believing that any unit of the State was capable of such things, Orwell couldn't conceive that the leaders of the nation he loved would sanction atrocities akin to some of the Nazis' own crimes. Nor, perhaps, could he imagine that the IRD, with his friends Kirwan and Koestler vouching for it, could be anything other than a good soldier in the war against Stalinist totalitarianism. That he could think so while completing his portrait of an even worse and more insidious form of tyranny may be the greatest paradox of an often very paradoxical person.

VIII. "THE ACT OF STANDING ASIDE"

Comfort shared Orwell's tendency to look at political events through a moral lens. But unlike his older friend, Comfort was relentlessly consistent in the positions he took. He was sometimes terribly unfair and unkind to people who enlisted or devoted themselves to government service during the war only because they passionately wanted to defeat fascism. He failed to see that war with Nazi Germany had changed the political dynamic and that defeating Hitler would require some terrible measures. He either failed to see or chose to look past the difference between other conflicts and war with a totalitarian system like Nazism, and he failed to consider that whatever the faults of Churchill's War Cabinet, it was fighting to liberate Europe from probably the most murderous tyranny in human history. Orwell was able to swallow his great aversion to Stalin in the cause of ending Nazism; Comfort was unwilling to amend any of his principles, even in the early years of the war, when Britain was virtually alone in carrying on the struggle.

This difference was partly a matter of personality and temperament: Orwell was a persistent self-critic, Comfort less so. Age may have had something to do with it as well.

Cynicism is often easier for the young, who haven't faced the need to make so many compromises; Comfort, still in his twenties, was perhaps too young to have gained this perspective. If, like Orwell, he had personally experienced the Spanish Civil War, including the Axis brand of warfare and the ruthless elimination of rivals that the Soviet leadership practiced—and not just the cancellation of his play—he might have found it harder to criticize Orwell's political choices. Later on, Comfort came to understand this; in "1939 and 1984," he responded to Orwell's later critics by describing his old adversary and friend as "a man unsparing of himself, facing excruciating moral decisions (as we all were) in the dark."[1]

But Orwell and Comfort differed in a perhaps more important way, which comes back to the question that initiated their quarrel: What is the right and appropriate way for a writer or artist to respond to war?

Orwell had "been trained for duty," V. S. Pritchett later remarked, and his response to the new European war reflected this.[2] "I had come to Spain with some notion of writing newspaper articles," he famously stated in the opening pages of *Homage to Catalonia*, "but I had joined the militia almost immediately, because at the time and in that atmosphere it seemed the only conceivable thing to do."[3] In January 1940, the war with Germany underway but the invasion of France still months in the future, the onetime quasi-pacifist wrote to a friend, "Now that we are in this bloody war we have to win & I would like to lend a hand."[4]

In a period of moral and physical emergency, Orwell looked for a way to serve: to determine the right side and volunteer himself for duty, to put his particularity as an individual aside in service to the cause. He might have hated the propaganda work he was assigned; in his diary he complained, "You can go on and on telling lies, and the most palpable lies at that, and even if they are not actually believed, there is no strong revulsion. We are all drowning in filth." Yet the work had to be done.[5]

"Filth," with the strong undercurrent of moral degradation it conveys, was an insult Alex Comfort often hurled at politicians who inflicted death on people, communities, and civilization and then routinely rationalized it. But Comfort's point of departure, as both a creative writer and a political actor, was different from Orwell's. Raised by parents who were minimally religious if at all, he was drawn to the Congregational Church in his late teens; his intention, on switching from classics to medicine at Cambridge, was to become a medical missionary. Simultaneously, his political development was moving in the direction of pacifism and anarchism. By the time he finished his studies and was engaging in his dispute with Orwell, his religious faith was waning and he was evolving toward the anarchism, blended with scientific humanism, he would adhere to for the rest of his life. But he detected continuity between the two. In a radio address on the BBC in 1949, "Is Christianity True?," he noted several things that modern, rationalistic people retain from "the old tradition": "the valuation of man for himself, and the individual as an individual . . . in the belief in the wide significance of what we do and what we think."[6]

Orwell would likely have agreed with this. Like Comfort, he derived a good deal of his ethics from his Christian upbringing. His "notion of decency was, in fact, the essence of the Christian morality, stripped of its superstitious and ascetic qualities," says Orwell scholar Kristian Williams.[7] He even retained a place in his heart for the Church of England: he was buried according to the rites of the church, following his request, in an English country churchyard. Big Brother's violation of the individual is the most morally obscene aspect of *Nineteen Eighty-Four*, and the care with which Winston Smith is "rehabilitated" testifies to the regime's understanding that "what we do and what we think" is crucially important, however much it tries to crush us physically.

Why would Big Brother devote so much attention to the case of one insignificant functionary? Why not just execute Winston Smith at once and deposit him down the memory hole? Orwell doesn't tell us specifically, but one possible answer points to another aspect of Judeo-Christian tradition that Comfort—and, perhaps, Orwell—appeared to have retained.

To "bear witness" is a concept with deep roots in Hebrew prophecy, where it implies disturbing the peace when matters do not conform to God's expectation. Doing so is one of the central duties of an active Christian, starting with the disciples and their mission to "witness" the revelation they had received in Jesus Christ. But to witness was never a synonym for preaching or exhorting others to believe or for merely passing on evidence of what one had seen. It had to be personal, informed by one's own experience and expressing one's own perception, and it had to touch on something eternal, not subject to the contradictory currents of a changing world. "Witness," in this sense, was how Christians supported each other in their faith.[8]

As religion loosened its grip on people in the West, the concept was translated into other realms of personal and public life, including the moral language of pacifism and, by way of the African American church, the American civil rights movement. "In the church in which I was raised you were supposed to bear witness to the truth," James Baldwin wrote.[9]

From the earliest years of his work in the movement, Martin Luther King Jr. linked his theology to his activism by arguing that Christians had a duty to bear witness for love and justice against evil.[10] American pacifists who organized around the War Resisters League in the postwar decades, notably during the Vietnam War, including A.J.

Muste, David Dellinger, David McReynolds, and Daniel and Philip Berrigan, took essentially the same position.

In *Nineteen Eighty-Four*, to destroy the impulse to bear witness—and to perfect the technique for doing so—is critical to the Inner Party's strategy for achieving permanence. That's why O'Brien is willing to devote so much care to Winston Smith's rehabilitation. And when Comfort spoke of the need for individuals to behave in a responsible manner, in both a positive and a negative sense, he was essentially speaking of their duty to bear witness. He and Orwell agreed that opposition to inhumanity had to originate and remain centered in the individual; they disagreed—and this was one of the few possibly unbridgeable gulfs between them—on Comfort's conviction that, however right and urgent the cause, this opposition must not use the same tools that tyrants use to maintain obedience.

Almost by definition, bearing witness meant revealing or insisting on inconvenient truths—the ones everyone else was too busy with seemingly more urgent matters to address. War was a great evil that damaged society in ways that extended far beyond the immediate effects of the violence. The fact that one side was less murderous than the other did not erase or postpone the duty to oppose it. This was one of those inconvenient truths.

The artist plays a central role here. "In essence," Comfort wrote in *Art and Social Responsibility*, "art is the act of standing aside from society." The responsibility of the artist or writer is to stand "far enough away from his subject to be able to see it in a reasonable and historical proportion," which is why "the right to stand aside is contested everywhere."

> Leaders who have acclaimed the work of a particular artist because he denounced their opponents are exasperated to find that the denunciatory criticism extends to them. [In the face of this,] we apply the same

standards to every cause or body which presents itself, without allegiance to any of them. We recognize
boundless responsibility to men, especially to all those
who are deprived of their voices, but ultimately to all
men, since they will in time become silent. We must
demand the right to secession as the one square foot of
ground which is solid and from which we can look and
interpret the gigantic chaos of human existence. We are
learning ourselves to live in the structure of insane societies while defying them.[11]

Baldwin, writing of his experiences in the South during the
civil right era, noted, "I was to discover that the line which
separates a witness from an actor is a very thin line indeed."[12]

Asserting his right to stand aside and then doing
everything he could to call attention to his government's
campaign of terror against enemy populations was what
Comfort's perceived responsibility—his duty to bear witness—told him he must do. Against the objection that in
the face of Nazism, the time for principled but probably
quixotic stands by individuals was over, Comfort insisted
that this is never the case because the actions that "our"
side takes during the war, both good and bad, will shape the
world we inherit from the conflict. It is not known whether
he had read *Homage to Catalonia*—most probably he did
at a later time—but, if so, he would have found his argument bolstered by Orwell's account of Soviet opportunism
and brutality in the service, allegedly, of antifascism.

In Spain, Orwell had suffered personally for his decision to bear witness when the most powerful elements
of the Left insisted that defeating Franco's forces neces-
sitated eliminating their own weaker rivals; it may have
perplexed Comfort to find Orwell denouncing him for
bearing witness against his own government a few years
later. In the last years of the war against Hitler, Orwell was
more inclined to agree with Comfort that the way Britain

conducted the war was as important—or almost as important—as the enemy it was fighting. He noted with regret an incident in which an American soldier, originally an Austrian Jew, kicked a captured SS officer who was "only doubtfully sane."[13]

He was disturbed as well by a photo from liberated Paris of "two partially undressed women, with shaven heads and with swastikas painted on their faces, being led through the streets of Paris amid grinning onlookers," and in response he quoted Nietzsche—"He who fights too long against dragons becomes a dragon himself"[14]—an echo of Comfort's earlier comment that Hitler's greatest victory would be to persuade the British to adopt his methods.

As it happens, Orwell wrote this at roughly the same time he was dismissing Vera Brittain's demand that the war be conducted in a more "limited" or "humane" manner. He reconciled the two positions by arguing that the test of his country's humanity would be its ability to follow victory with magnanimity and reconciliation rather than revenge, even if the war itself had to be fought with no quarter. But is even this possible? States define themselves in opposition to other states; demonizing the enemy, denying the foe's humanity, is one way they legitimate their power. If Britain and the United States treated defeated Germany and Japan with relative magnanimity after 1945, it was only because the victors needed their help against a new Great Enemy: the Soviet Union. As an anarchist rather than a social democrat, Comfort may have had an easier time than Orwell understanding that many of the horrible practices the world encountered in Spain, in Germany and occupied Europe, and in Soviet Russia weren't entirely the product of a few very evil regimes, but resulted from the development of the State itself and would not go away with the defeat or collapse of those regimes.

The Orwell of *Nineteen Eighty-Four* understood this. Winston Smith's struggle is not with a particular state but with the State itself; by the time he's arrested near the end of the novel, he's close to actively opposing the entire system of mental conditioning Big Brother embodies. To maintain the robustness of that system, the regime must not just eliminate such enemies but "cure" them of the impulse to stand aside and bear witness.

Arguably, some aspects of Comfort's pacifist position were simplistic. Was everyone who signed on as a soldier, spy, bureaucrat, or broadcaster complicit in the atrocities the British government committed? Didn't the soldiers and embedded journalists bear witness when they liberated the Nazi death camps and reported what they saw to the world? And was their witness any less morally valuable than Comfort's because they wore a government-issue uniform? While it was all very well to valorize popular resistance forces, with a few exceptions such as Tito's partisans in Yugoslavia, any successes were counterbalanced by reprisals the German exacted against the subject population. Were these brave people really doing more valuable work than the enlisted soldiers dying by the thousands on conventional battlegrounds?

Nevertheless, to consider and call attention to the world being created by the war was a necessity, an extremely unpopular job that had to be done—and just as much a form of wartime service as the kind Orwell sought, even if it meant the opposite of supporting the "war effort."

In America, this becomes only too clear when we consider how the postwar world has been shaped by the rise of nuclear weapons, crafted by Washington in secret, with no chance for the public to debate the wisdom of doing so; by the predominant place assigned to air war, notably in the drone raids of our time; by the rise of the national security state, with its mania for secrecy and covert action; by the blanketing of the globe with U.S. military bases and special operations forces; by the rise of the military-industrial complex; and by the militarization of domestic policing. All of these developments can be traced, directly or indirectly, to the transformation of the State during World War II. They've occurred both in dictatorships and in democracies.

Ironically, *Nineteen Eighty-Four* itself can be seen to bolster this perspective. Winston Smith's personal rebellion was, in the eyes of his fellow citizens and the State, an act of irresponsibility at a time when his country was—supposedly—engaged in a life-or-death struggle with another superpower. The novel offers an extended demonstration of how cleverly the State can manufacture a condition of permanent crisis and then pervert the individual's search for "the only conceivable thing to do"—precisely what occurred during the Cold War and, later, the War on Terror. In much of his postwar journalism, Orwell assumed that the Cold War was the same type of conflict, on a moral level, as World War II; in his greatest novel, he suggests that it may not have been.

IX. CONCLUSION

The issues that separated—and united—these two very different figures would follow them for many decades: Comfort into his later career as a scientist, activist, and writer, and Orwell through the twists and turns of his posthumous reputation. But the differences between them lay not just in the positions they took on issues or the way they worked through them; one of the most important dividing lines was how each chose to be political and the arenas in which he chose to do so—and these were pretty well fixed by the time Orwell died.

After his service in the POUM militia in Spain, Orwell spent his active political life largely in more mainstream channels. He volunteered his services to the government during World War II and afterward attempted to aid the IRD in what he thought was a commendable effort to counter Soviet propaganda. While he agreed to serve on the Freedom Defence Committee, he was suspicious of the politics Comfort practiced, congenitally and because he thought it was ineffective. He couldn't abide eccentrics and personal nonconformists, who, he believed, would only alienate the middle class from socialism. In his *Partisan Review* attack on Comfort and other pacifists, for instance, he wrote bluntly of Gandhi's strategy of nonviolence, "Despotic governments can stand 'moral force' until the cows come home; what they fear is physical force."[1]

He was wrong, as the long-term success of Gandhi's nonviolent campaigns to delegitimize British rule in India proved. But when Orwell talked about the need to choose sides, he generally meant one state over another; there was always a right side and a wrong side in any such conflict, he presumed.

Comfort, by contrast, practiced an outsider politics, closer to Gandhi's and not tied to legal institutions or conventional methods of applying pressure. As an anarchist, he always advocated disobedience: agitating for change through strikes, demonstrations, and individual refusal to cooperate, seeing these methods as carrying the germ of a new society without the State.

Comfort was a fixture of the nuclear disarmament movement that grew up in postwar Britain, as both a public speaker and the author of a stream of articles and pamphlets, many of them published in *Freedom* and in *Peace News*, the publication of the PPU, of which he continued to be a member. The nuclear politics of the Cold War only reinforced his conviction that the leaders of the superpowers were delinquents at best and psychotics at worst. The geopolitical landscape was profoundly different from what it had been during World War II, he argued at a 1951 event organized by the London Anarchist Group. The speech was then reprinted in *Freedom*:

> The people who are most certain of Russia's warlike intentions are not enemies of tyranny. They did not stop Syngman Rhee's executions [in Korea], or deplore Chiang's police state [in China, then Taiwan]. They have not scrupled to collect and uphold a long series of discreditable tyrannies. . . . I could respect, though I could not support, anyone who thought that armed

force might be used today to liberate someone, either
from abuses in the East or from abuses in the West. That
is not today. War will liberate nobody from anything.
If we co-operate with it in any shape or form, we shall
place ourselves in the hands of men as devoted, through
their own fears, to the commission of unlimited and
purposeless crime as were the Nazis—more unlimited
and more purposeless.[2]

This connects directly to the fundamental question that
pacifism asks: If not now, when? Every war is sold to the
people who must bear the burden as a step on the road to
lasting peace—another "war to end all wars." Opposing
this war, then, is never permissible, and so war is peace,
as Orwell said. But oppose it we must, since war—even
a "good" one—kills millions, destroys communities, and
reinforces authoritarian tendencies in society and its leaders. One way to oppose war is to break down the barriers
between the people of the hostile states. During the Cold
War, Comfort and others believed the danger of nuclear
annihilation made it urgent for intellectuals, scientists, and
activists to build bridges between the societies on either
side of the Iron Curtain, regardless of the animosity between their governments.

In September 1954, in the years leading to the post-
Stalin Thaw, Comfort was one of a group of British
physicians who made a three-week tour of the Soviet
Union, visiting medical and psychiatric facilities and meeting with their counterparts there. Subsequently, as his
gerontological work gained prominence, Comfort attended scientific and medical conferences regularly in Russia
and Eastern Europe, forming a number of professional
friendships in the field. One of the closest of these was
with Zhores Medvedev, the Soviet gerontologist and dis-
sident. Comfort smuggled several of Medvedev's samizdat
manuscripts out of the Eastern Bloc and helped get them

published in the UK; after Medvedev was stripped of his Soviet citizenship in London in 1972, Comfort helped him settle and find work in Britain.[3]

What would Orwell have made of this? He grasped the dangers of a nuclear-inflected global politics, but would he have approved of Comfort's efforts to bring Western and Soviet scientists together? And would he have appreciated the choices that the Cold War imposed on Comfort and other British opponents of the Bomb?

Orwell's political home during the 1940s, to the extent he had one, was in the left wing of the Labour Party, whose voice in the media was *Tribune* and whose most prominent public face was that of Aneurin Bevan, the Welsh social democrat who created the National Health Service as minister of health in the Attlee Government following the war. But as the Cold War ground on, Labour moved slowly but surely into conformity with the anti-Soviet policies of Britain's U.S. ally. To the dismay of antinuclear activists, Bevan, who had previously supported their demand that Britain unilaterally scrap its nuclear arsenal, reversed himself in 1957, arguing that otherwise "it would send a British Foreign Secretary naked into the conference-chamber" with the Soviets.

Comfort joined the Campaign for Nuclear Disarmament (CND) soon after it was launched in 1958. Shortly before, Comfort had also joined a more militant group, the Direct Action Committee against Nuclear War (DAC). The CND still attempted to work through the Labour Party to secure unilateral disarmament while the DAC opted to work outside mainstream politics, building its strategy around marches, rallies, and civil disobedience. In 1958, the two groups worked together, a bit uneasily, to stage a march from Trafalgar Square to Aldermaston, site of the government's nuclear weapons research facility. Thereafter, with the route reversed, the Aldermaston march became an annual event, marking the birth of a new protest politics in the UK. It was also an incubator of the 1960s counterculture in that country.

Comfort worked equally for both groups: writing, speaking throughout the country, even writing songs for marchers and setting up a solo pirate radio station to broadcast the antinuclear message (it reached very few people, and they heard mostly static). But in 1960, impatient with what they felt was the CND's disinclination to ruffle the establishment's feathers, Comfort joined Bertrand Russell and other members as well as the DAC to form the Committee of 100, which aimed to mount a campaign of civil disobedience. The committee's high-water mark came in September 1961 when it staged a mass sit-down demonstration in Trafalgar Square that attracted twelve thousand participants.

Comfort was not among them. He and thirty-five other committee members, including Russell, had earlier been charged with inciting "divers persons unknown unlawfully to obstruct the highway at or in the vicinity of Parliament Square." They were presented with the choice either to be "bound over," that is, to pledge good behavior for the next twelve months, avoiding the Trafalgar Square event and staying away from any other such occasions, or be imprisoned. Comfort and thirty-one others refused to be bound over and were sentenced just before the sit-down was to take place—Comfort was sentenced to one month in prison, reduced to one week after he paid a fine of twenty-five pounds.

Comfort continued for the rest of his active life to identify as an anarchist, to write and speak against nuclear weapons, and to link disarmament with his opposition to the growing authoritarian streak in the Western democracies. In 1986, after his return to Thatcherite Britain from twelve years living in the United States, Comfort wrote a "Letter after America" (the title evokes Orwell's wartime "London Letters" to *Partisan Review*) for the centenary edition of *Freedom* celebrating the hundredth anniversary of Freedom Press. In the piece, he noted some things he was dismayed to discover about the country of his birth:

> It is distinctly strange to find oneself living in a colonial country, with armed police, lathi-charges* and trumped-up charges as appropriate responses to trade unions, and the promise of rubber bullets to come. . . . What is new to British history is the shadow of the [Ferdinand] Marcos pattern: a country full of foreign troops and foreign nuclear bases, with a client government drawing its support and its guidelines from Washington.[4]

Like many postwar European intellectuals, Comfort believed—still—that his country's interests ultimately "involve neutrality, and the neutralisation of Europe." That meant nuclear disarmament and opting out of NATO and the Soviet-American Cold War. "Accidents apart, this will eventually happen," he wrote. In more than four decades, his overall political perspective had changed very little, and, in this, he poses a stark contrast to Orwell. Often hailed for his moral consistency, Orwell in fact was quite often at war with himself, which is partly why he remains such an interesting character. A mini-industry, featuring almost as many sectarian divisions as there are among Marxian scholars, still works at divining the political direction he would have taken had he lived, replaying the controversy that began with Orwell's first writings on Spain in 1938.

After the war, however, Comfort never denounced or abandoned Orwell; he took over *Tribune*'s "As I Please" column on at least one occasion after Orwell ceased writing it.[5] And it is likely that Comfort and Orwell would have ended up largely in agreement on at least one key issue. "In Defence of Comrade Zilliacus,"** an article Orwell wrote in

---

*   Baton charges by police in British India to break up crowds and demonstrations.
**   The title refers to a then well-known Labour MP and Soviet apologist.

1947–1948 but that was only published long after his death, advocated a third way for Europe not dissimilar from the one Comfort later suggested: "We are no longer strong enough to stand alone, and if we fail to bring a West European union into being we shall be obliged, in the long run, to subordinate our policy to that of one Great Power or another." A little more explicitly, he wrote, "Therefore a Socialist United States of Europe seems to me the only worthwhile political objective today."[6] The U.S., of course, was firmly opposed to such an idea.

Yet there was still the Orwell who expected to side with the Americans if push came to shove. As a result, many people on the left—many but not all with pro-Soviet leanings—could not forgive him for the Manichaean view he took of East-West relations from 1945 onward. During the Vietnam War, the antiwar Left and much of the media worked to expose America's atrocities rather than downplay them—something only a few outliers were willing to risk during World War II. While the Vietnam War was raging, Mary McCarthy wrote of Orwell, plausibly, "I can hear him angrily arguing that to oppose the Americans in Vietnam, whatever their shortcomings, is to be 'objectively' totalitarian," echoing Orwell's wartime attacks on pacifists like Comfort.[7] Norman Podhoretz argued in 1983 that Orwell was "a forerunner of neoconservatism" and that if he were alive then, at age eighty, he would have been a dyed-in-the-wool anticommunist.[8]

Not everyone agreed. Despite his doubts about Gandhi, one of the few completely consistent political positions Orwell held throughout his career was that the European colonial empires must be dismantled—a stand that would have made it difficult for him to support the Vietnam War or any other effort to push back against anticolonial insurgencies.

"Orwell stood much nearer to the Anarchists, like Godwin and Proudhon, who contended that the organization of society must be inspired by moral vision, than to the Socialists," Woodcock concluded in *The Crystal Spirit*, his study of Orwell.[9]

This is a valid point, and it is the fundamental link between Orwell's thinking and Comfort's. But Orwell's intellectual affinities with anarchism ran deeper, whether he knew it or not. Pierre-Joseph Proudhon, the pioneering nineteenth-century French anarchist theorist, may have originated the politics of the absurd when he argued that any idea, taken to its extreme, will contradict itself. "The majority of ideas which govern us, through until their last consequences, are destructive of their object and contradict themselves," he wrote. "Thus, property becomes theft, government tyranny, competition privilege, community itself becomes property again, etc."[10]

This is the same logical absurdity Orwell described in *Animal Farm*, when Napoleon re-enslaves the animals and turns the farm back into a capitalist enterprise, and it foreshadows even more strongly the slogans that bombard the citizens of Oceania in *Nineteen Eighty-Four*: War Is Peace, Freedom Is Slavery, Ignorance Is Strength.

The anarchist writer and publisher Nicolas Walter called Orwell "the best anti-militarist we ever had" and predicted that if he had lived, with the prospect of the Bomb still hanging over his head, he might have "returned to his old anti-militarism."[11] Even McCarthy wasn't totally convinced by her own argument: "The word protest would have made him sick. . . . As for the student revolt, he might have been out of sympathy for a dozen reasons, but would he have sympathized with the administrators? If he had lived he might have been happiest on a desert island, and it was a blessing for him probably that he died."[12]

In a sense, this is exactly what Orwell did, living most of his last years on the remote Scottish island of Jura. But the truth about Orwell lies somewhere between McCarthy's and Woodcock's assertions. *Nineteen*

Eighty-Four may be Orwell's greatest achievement, but it also marked a kind of impasse. He was ready to take the side of the United States in the Cold War rather than risk a world molded by Stalin, but he feared that the Cold War could easily turn into a live conflict that would rip apart the fabric of cultures and communities, creating the kind of vacuum into which Big Brother could step. The appendix on "The Principles of Newspeak" that ends *Nineteen Eighty-Four* implies that the Inner Party's project would ultimately fail and its tyranny would come to an end, some time before 2050. But how that would happen is left hanging.

Orwell was always looking for the answer, even if he was never fully satisfied with what he found. In 1946, he wrote a series of articles for the *Manchester Evening News*, collectively entitled "The Intellectual Revolt," in which he surveyed what he considered to be the most intriguing nonmainstream political tendencies of the time: utopian and nonauthoritarian socialists, Christian reformers, individualist free-market defenders such as the economist Friedrich Hayek, idiosyncratic radicals such as Bertrand Russell and Aldous Huxley—and pacifists, whom he lumped in and sometimes conflated with anarchists. Some were reformists, some objected to all government, some "want only to pursue a simple, natural life," but a connecting thread wove through all these groups, Orwell argued: "opposition to the tyranny of the State" and to "the values of the Machine Age."[13]

The four articles are among the most interesting Orwell produced in the postwar years because they brought into focus, before the fact, some of the major influences on the new political culture of the 1960s and beyond: anti-militarism, environmentalism, anarchism, free-market libertarianism, and a simultaneous fascination with and fear of technology. Orwell summarized the basic position of anarchists like Comfort and Read reasonably well:

> Civilization now rests upon force. It rests not only on
> guns and bombing planes, but on prisons, concentra-
> tion camps, and the policeman's truncheon. . . . [But] the
> use of force makes real progress impossible. The good
> society is one in which human beings are equal and in
> which they co-operate with one another willingly and
> not because of fear or economic compulsion.[14]

When Orwell tried to encapsulate pacifism and the
attitude of anarchists toward technology, however, he over-
simplified. At some point, the pacifist believes, the cycle
of violence must be broken: "even at the cost of accepting
defeat and foreign domination, we must begin to act pa-
cifically and refuse to return evil for evil." Comfort, who
strongly supported the right of the occupied to use force
against the occupier, would not have recognized himself in
this statement. "On the whole, the direction of anarchist
thought is toward a kind of primitivism," Orwell continued.[15] As a scientist who believed that scientific knowledge
was critical to human liberation, Comfort would have vig-
orously disagreed.

But Orwell ended his article on pacifism with an
indication that he understood the value of the anarchist position and sympathized with it, up to a point: "They have
rightly insisted that present-day society, even when the
guns do not happen to be firing, is not peaceful, and they
have kept alive the idea—somewhat neglected since the
Russian Revolution—that the aim of progress is to abolish
the authority of the State and not to strengthen it."[16]

These were the thoughts Orwell was pursuing even as
he assembled his notebook of ideological unreliables—and
they are very far from the "mutual arse-licking" of which
he had accused pacifists just a few years before. Woodcock,
who was close to him in his last years, wrote, "Anarchism
remained a restless presence in his mind right to the end;
it was one of the themes he hoped to develop in the novels

after the manner of Joseph Conrad which, when he died, he was planning as his program for work in the 1950's."[17]

Had Orwell lived to pursue this project, very likely he would again have encountered Alex Comfort. During the war, Comfort had argued that the roots of a freer and wiser postwar culture lay in the experience of defeat, not victory, in indigenous wartime resistance and noncooperation, not patriotism. His statement of this position in *Horizon* was the provocation for Orwell to attack him in *Partisan Review*. But the wartime and postwar writings of Albert Camus (to whom Orwell sent a copy of *Animal Farm* and who would be a powerful influence on Comfort's writings), Irène Némirovsky, Jean-Paul Sartre, Heinrich Böll, Simone de Beauvoir, Günter Grass, Siegfried Lenz, Peter Weiss, Jerzy Andrzejewski, Tadeusz Borowski, Dietrich Bonhoeffer, Rolf Hochhuth, Carlo Levi, Vasily Grossman, Shohei Ooka, Jerzy Kosinski, André Schwarz-Bart, Primo Levi, Patrick Modiano, and other writers who bore witness to the invasion or defeat of their country or the destruction of their people, suggests that Comfort was largely correct. Very little produced by British or American wartime writers, who never saw their nations occupied and humiliated, reaches the same level of achievement. *Nineteen Eighty-Four* is one of the exceptions, and it can be seen as a partial acceptance of Comfort's argument: a novel of universal defeat written from the vantage point of one of the war's victors.

But Orwell, had he lived, would also have faced a far less tidy political landscape than the one he encountered in the years of struggle against fascism. Thanks in part to nuclear weapons, the Cold War blossomed into an existential threat to humanity that the United States and its allies did at least as much as the Soviet bloc to enhance. There have been no more global conflicts like World War II and very few conventional wars of the traditional sort. Instead, both during and after the Cold War, we have had "conflicts": civil wars, proxy wars, regional power struggles, insurgencies, counterinsurgencies, ethnic and religious pogroms, struggles for decolonization, and spurious "police actions" such as the invasions of Grenada and Panama, the Soviet and American invasions of Afghanistan, and the numerous proxy campaigns, "advisory" missions, and drone assaults the United States has carried out since the terrorist attacks of September 2001. Even a full-scale conventional assault like the U.S. invasion of Iraq quickly transformed into another drawn-out counterinsurgency in which no side wins but noncombatants suffer endlessly. Very few of these were formally declared "wars," but collectively they have been just as brutal, devastating, and in some cases genocidal.

In this context, the questions Comfort and the anarcho-pacifists persistently raised during World War II seem more contemporary than those Orwell posed about the failure to put aside one's skepticism in the face of a war against absolute evil. Comfort's argument that indigenous resistance movements like the Maquis held the key to a new society may have seemed naive at the time, but today, similar grassroots movements may be among our best hopes. The Zapatistas in Mexico, the autonomous cantons of Rojava in Syria, and even, in a very different setting, the sanctuary cities movement in the United States responding to the Trump administration's attacks on undocumented immigrants may seem ragtag and uncoordinated. Yet they not only offer beleaguered people some command over their fate but also hold out the hope of building a collective consciousness that offers an alternative to what both Orwell and Comfort saw as an increasingly grim and straitened future.

Orwell's attacks on pacifism seem dated as well. He may have been speaking for the majority of the British and American public when he dismissed Vera Brittain's pleadings to "humanize" the war as "humbug," but he was wrong that "no decent person cares tuppence for posterity." The consequences of the war as it was being fought, and how these would determine the shape of warfare and international rivalries in the postwar period, were exactly what Brittain, Comfort, and others were most concerned about—and so, increasingly, was the British public as victory came within sight and the national sense of immediate danger receded.

Revulsion against actions like the Dresden raid was such that at the war's end a separate campaign medal was not created for Bomber Command's crews. That decision prompted their chief, Bomber Harris, to refuse an offered peerage—he was the only one of the major British warlords not to accept one—and to complain in his autobiography, with reason, that the criticism over Dresden was coming from "a good many people who admit that our earlier attacks were as fully justified as any other operation of war."[18]

Of the sixty million estimated to have died in World War II, some fifty to fifty-five million were civilians. And while these numbers were not widely known in the years immediately following the war, it was clear to many people in proximity to the fighting that warfare was mutating into a form of mass extermination. In 1949, the Fourth Geneva Convention was concluded, establishing protections for civilians in time of war, outlawing collective punishment, and stating flatly, "No protected person may be punished for an offense he or she has not personally committed."

Today the Fourth Geneva Convention is considered to have passed into the body of customary international law, which means that even nonsignatories are bound by its provisions. In 1977, an additional protocol outlawed indiscriminate attacks on civilian populations as well as destruction of food, water, and other materials needed for survival—including by use of technology such as biological weapons, nuclear weapons, and land mines. In October 2017, the Nobel Peace Prize was awarded to the International Campaign to Abolish Nuclear Weapons, which helped drive negotiation of the first treaty to prohibit nuclear arms.

The United States—the only remaining superpower—is one of at least a half-dozen states that have not ratified the additional protocol, and it has shown no interest in signing the nuclear ban treaty. For the most part, the Convention is disregarded. Governments in Washington and elsewhere have continued to torture and terrorize civilian populations as a routine part of war-making.

Only a few years after Germany and Japan's surrender, the United States intervened in a civil war between Communist and non-Communist regimes in Korea. It began a sustained airborne assault that included bombing cities, towns, and villages and incinerating them with napalm. "Over a period of three years, we killed off—what—20% of the population," General Curtis LeMay, then head of the U.S. Strategic Air Command, said years later. The Northern capital of Pyongyang was almost completely eviscerated; all but two buildings were destroyed in a city that was once home to more than a half-million people. Other targets included vital civilian infrastructure such as hydroelectric and irrigation dams. Twice annually, the United States and South Korea perform war games aimed at updating their preparations for an invasion from the North. Activities include a simulated nuclear first strike against North Korea with dummy munitions.[19]

More recently—the examples are many—Britain, France, and the United States orchestrated an air war over Libya aimed at supporting rebels fighting to remove Qaddafi from power. From August 2011 to April 2012, according to Human Rights Watch, NATO conducted some ninety-seven hundred sorties and dropped over seventy-seven hundred bombs on Libya. More than one-third hit civilian targets; in some cases, HRW could identify no legitimate military target. The attacks killed at least seventy-two civilians, one-third of them children under age eighteen.[20] The power vacuum the NATO attacks helped create destroyed Libya as a functioning political entity, ushering in a civil war that continues as of this writing.

While the Geneva Conventions' protections for civilians are now part of humanity's moral code, the destruction of civilian populations remains a basic tool of warfare. States still wage airborne "shock and awe" campaigns. But public opposition has been a persistent thorn in their sides, which is why our commanders in chief continue to insist—against the evidence, just as the Air Ministry did during World War II—that they only carry out "pinpoint," "surgical" strikes against legitimate military targets.

One reason, perhaps, is that air wars never really end: the evidence is always there to remind us. In September 2017, the city of Frankfurt evacuated more than sixty

Stuttgart, August 16, 2017: An unexploded 250-kg aerial bomb was discovered during construction work and defused that night.
Photo: Sdmg/Werner/SDMG/dpa/Alamy Live News

thousand residents from their homes while experts defused a leftover, four-thousand-pound British bomb. About 10 percent of the city's population was affected. Four months earlier, some forty thousand were evacuated in Hannover when three unexploded RAF bombs were found. ("The city has set up a programme of museum tours, children's films and sporting events to help evacuees spend the day as pleasantly as possible," the BBC reported.) In a similar event in 2010 in Göttingen, three members of a bomb disposal squad were killed.[21] More than seventy years after the war ended, over two thousand tons of unexploded weaponry still turn up every year in Germany—almost always in dense urban areas.*

Just as it no longer seems absurd to protest the worst aspects of modern warfare, Comfort's skepticism of Churchill and his cohort appears more understandable today, given the doubts that millions around the world harbored in 2003 when George W. Bush and his aides decided they were the right people to oust the tyrant of Baghdad and bring peace and democracy to the Middle East. Churchill was not Bush, and certainly defeating the Axis was an enormous and imperative task while the U.S. invasion of Iraq was nothing of the sort. But the outcome of World War II was the Cold War, the competitive production and refinement of nuclear arms, the surveillance state, and the continuing suppression of popular movements by governments anxious to press their advantage, or at least to preserve the status quo.

If anything, the State has become more ruthless and more prone to deception than it was when Comfort and Orwell wrote. Certainly, its leaders are just as apt to take actions that in other contexts would be considered

---

*   Germany's postwar political and business leaders bear some of the blame: "In the rush to rebuild after the war, Germans often just buried the munitions, so many of them are only turning up now." Edmund Heaphy, "Frankfurt Evacuates 60,000 People over Bomb Dropped Seven Decades Ago," *New York Times*, September 4, 2017.

sociopathic—with legislative acts like the Authorization for Use of Military Force (in the case of the United States) to protect them from prosecution. And they are just as likely to lie about their conduct as was the Air Ministry when it denied bombing civilians during World War II. In February 2017, we learned that the Pentagon, which had pledged not to use PGU-14, a 30mm depleted-uranium bullet, in its war against the Islamic State in Syria, had in fact used thousands of rounds of the shells, with their attendant health risks.[22] In December of that year, an Associated Press investigation found that some 9,000–11,000 civilians were killed in the bloody, nine-month assault against Islamic State forces in Mosul—ten times more than official estimates. Neither the Iraqi government, the U.S.-led coalition, nor the Islamic State itself would acknowledge the

Graffiti at drone bombing site, Sana'a, Yemen, February 6, 2017.
Photo: Khaled Abdullah, Reuters

numbers, even though most of them came from Mosul's morgue. "It was the biggest assault on a city in a couple of generations, all told," said Chris Woods, head of Airwars, an independent group that documented air and artillery attacks in Iraq and Syria.[23]

If Comfort were alive, these revelations would have shocked but not surprised him, registering as yet another example of the irresponsibility of the State, carrying us one step further in the decline of sociability and another step toward barbarism. His answer would doubtless be the same one he offered during World War II and the nuclear buildup of the postwar decades: Be responsible. Disobey.

Orwell, if he were alive, might look back on the war and the period of his quarrel with Comfort as a simpler time, when the Enemy could be an individual, a political party, or a particular nation, but not the State itself. He shared many of Comfort's misgivings, as we have seen, but except in the pages of *Nineteen Eighty-Four*, he generally chose to suppress or downplay these in the belief that helping defeat Hitler and later Stalin was his overriding duty, at least at that moment. Out of just as strong a sense of duty, Comfort chose to express his fears loudly. But Orwell and Comfort both, for similar reasons, dreaded the world that would follow the war almost as much as the war itself. They were right.

ENDNOTES

Chapter I: The Moral Lens

1   George Orwell, "War-time Diary," March 14, 1942, in *The Collected Essays, Journalism and Letters of George Orwell*, vol. 2: *My Country Right or Left, 1940–1943*, ed. Sonia Orwell and Ian Angus (London: Penguin, 1968), 465.

2   Alex Comfort, "October, 1944," *NOW* 4 (1944).

3   Alex Comfort, "1939 and 1984: George Orwell and the Vision of Judgment," in *On Nineteen Eighty-Four*, ed. Peter Stansky (New York: W. H. Freeman, 1983), 16.

4   Quoted in George Orwell, "No, Not One," review of *No Such Liberty*, by Alex Comfort, *Adelphi*, October 1941.

5   Included in *The Lost Orwell: Being a Supplement to the Complete Works of George Orwell*, compiled and annotated by Peter Davison (London: Timewell, 2006), 142.

6   Timothy Garton Ash, "Love, Death and Treachery," *Guardian Review*, June 21, 2003; author interview with Nicholas Comfort, November 21, 2016.

Chapter II: A Clash of Temperaments

1   George Orwell, "London Letter," *Partisan Review*, March–April 1942.

2   Randolph Bourne, "War and the Intellectuals," *Seven Arts*, June 1917.

3   George Orwell, "Politics vs. Literature: An Examination of

Gulliver's Travels," *Polemic,* no. 5 (September 1946).

4   Alex Comfort, "A Controversy," *Partisan Review,* September–October 1942.

5   Bernard Crick, *George Orwell: A Life* (London: Secker & Warburg, 1980), 308.

6   George Woodcock, *The Crystal Spirit: A Study of George Orwell* (New York: Minerva, 1966), 303.

7   John Rodden, *The Politics of Literary Reputation: The Making and Claiming of "St. George Orwell"* (New York: Oxford University Press, 1988), 94.

8   Paul Flewers, "'I Know How, but I Don't Know Why': George Orwell's Conception of Totalitarianism," in *George Orwell: Enigmatic Socialist,* collected by Paul Flewers (London: Socialist Platform, 2005), 8.

9   George Orwell, "Patriots and Revolutionaries," in *The Betrayal of the Left,* ed. Victor Gollancz (London, 1941), 234–45, cited in Paul Flewers, "I Know How, but I Don't Know Why," in *George Orwell: Enigmatic Socialist,* 10.

10   Alex Comfort, interview by David Goodway, March 16, 1989.

11   George Orwell, "English Poetry Since 1900," broadcast June 13, 1943, in *Orwell: The War Broadcasts,* ed. W. J. West (London: Duckworth, 1985), 127–29.

12   George Orwell, letter to Alex Comfort, July 11, 1943, in *George Orwell: A Life in Letters,* ed. Peter Davison (New York: Liveright, 2010), 213.

13   Quoted in Simon Leys, "The Intimate Orwell," *New York Review of Books,* May 26, 2011.

14   Woodcock, *Crystal Spirit,* 14; George Orwell, 1938 letter to Stephen Spender, cited in Bernard Crick, *George Orwell: A Life* (Boston: Little, Brown, 1980), 243.

15   George Orwell, "A Controversy," *Partisan Review,* September–October 1942.

16   Jeffrey Meyers, *Orwell: Wintry Conscience of a Generation* (New York: W. W. Norton, 2000), 201.

17   George Orwell, review of *The Men I Killed,* by Brigadier-General F. P. Crozier, *New Statesman and Nation,* August 28, 1937.

18   D. J. Taylor, *Orwell: The Life* (New York: Henry Holt, 2003), 263.

19   George Orwell, letter to Herbert Read, March 5, 1939, in *The Collected Essays, Journalism and Letters of George Orwell,* vol. 1: *An Age Like This, 1920–1940,* ed. Sonia Orwell and Ian Angus

(London: Secker & Warburg, 1968), 385–87.

20   Review of *Communism and Man* by F. J. Sheed, *Peace News*, January 27, 1939.

21   Taylor, *Orwell: The Life*, 272.

22   Richard Overy, "Pacifism and the Blitz, 1940–1941," *Past and Present*, no. 219 (May 2013): 202–5.

23   Richard Overy, email to the author, September 27, 2017.

24   Richard Overy, "Constructing Space for Dissent in War: The Bombing Restriction Committee, 1941–1945," *English Historical Review* 131, no. 550 (2016): 598–99.

25   Quoted in Nicholson Baker, *Human Smoke: The Beginnings of World War II, the End of Civilization* (New York: Simon & Schuster, 2008), 152.

26   Richard Overy, "Constructing Space for Dissent," 599.

27   Baker, *Human Smoke*, 167.

28   Robin Neillands, *The Bomber War: The Allied Air Offensive Against Nazi Germany* (New York: Barnes and Noble, 2005), 38.

29   Richard Overy, email to author, September 27, 2017.

30   "Lake of Fire Seen at Wilhelmshaven," *New York Times*, January 17, 1941, cited in Baker, *Human Smoke*, 284. Civilian casualties in Wilhelmshaven only totaled 435, due to an extensive network of air raid shelters. "Traces of Evil: Remaining Nazi Sites in Germany," http://www.tracesofevil.com/search/label/Wilhelmshaven.

31   Richard Overy, email to author, September 27, 2017.

32   Richard Overy, *The Bombers and the Bombed: Allied Air War over Europe, 1940–1945* (New York: Penguin, 2015), 97–98, 260.

33   Overy, *Bombers and the Bombed*, 210–15. The number of homeless was cited in W. G. Sebald, "Air War and Literature," in *On the Natural History of Destruction* (New York: Random House, 2003), 3–4.

34   A. J. P. Taylor, *The Second World War* (London: Hamish Hamilton, 1975), 129.

35   Overy, *Bombers and the Bombed*, 58.

36   Quoted in Denis Richards, *The Royal Air Force*, vol. 1: *The Fight at Odds* (London: Her Majesty's Stationery Office, 1953), ch. 13, cited in Baker, *Human Smoke*, 355.

37   Charles Webster and Noble Frankland, *The Strategic Air Offensive against Germany, Vol. 4* (London: Her Majesty's Stationery Office, 1961), 137–41, cited in Baker, *Human Smoke*, 313.

38   Overy, "Constructing Space for Dissent," 611.

39   Overy, *Bombers and the Bombed*, 90–91.

40   Ibid., 198–99.

41   Anthony Bevoor, "The War on Every Front," *Wall Street*

Journal, October 25, 2017.

42   C. L. Sulzberger, "Famine Spread Menaces Greece," *New York Times*, July 2, 1941, cited in Baker, *Human Smoke*, 353.

43   "Feed Starving War Children, Hoover Pleads," *Chicago Tribune*, October 20, 1941, cited in Baker, *Human Smoke*, 411.

44   "French Speed Aid for Enemy Aliens," *New York Times*, December 17, 1939; and "France Interns 15,000 Germans," *New York Times*, September 19, 1939; both cited in Baker, *Human Smoke*, 141.

45   "PPU History in Context," Peace Pledge Union, http://www.ppu.org.uk/ppu/history1.html, cited in Baker, *Human Smoke*, 196.

46   Vanessa Redgrave, *An Autobiography* (New York: Random House, 1994), 26–28.

47   "1940–1949: Candles in the Dark," Peace Pledge Union, http://www.ppu.org.uk/century/century5.html, cited in Baker, *Human Smoke*, 196.

48   Tristana Moore, "Nazi Deserter Hails Long-Awaited Triumph," BBC News, September 8, 2009; Charles Hawley, "Germany Considers Rehabilitating Soldiers Executed for 'Treason,'" *Spiegel Online*, June 29, 2007; email from Richard Overy, September 27, 2017.

49   Overy, *Bombers and the Bombed*, 53.

50   Antony Beevor, *Stalingrad* (London: Penguin, 1998), 102–4.

51   See Frederick Taylor, *Coventry: Thursday, 14 November 1940* (New York: Bloomsbury, 2015), 68, 164.

Chapter III: A Public "Set-To"

1   "The Bombing of Civilians: Ending It by Agreement," Public Affairs News Service, September 1940.

2   Overy, "Constructing Space for Dissent," 602.

3   Overy, "Pacifism and the Blitz," 206.

4   Ibid., 229.

5   "Conscientious Objectors Founded Theatre," *Market Rasen Mail*, February 1, 2006; Sally Weale, "Utopia in Lincolnshire: The Pacifists Who Built a Farm – and Stayed," *Guardian*, December 5, 2017.

6   Christopher Isherwood, *Diaries: Vol. 1*, ed. Katherine Bucknell (New York: HarperCollins, 1996), 83–84.

7   Overy, "Pacifism and the Blitz," 219–20, 225.

8   Overy, "Constructing Space for Dissent," 610.

9   David Garnett, *War in the Air: September 1939–May 1941* (New York: Doubleday, Doran, 1941), 225–26, 269, cited in Baker, *Human Smoke*, 388.

10   George Orwell, "War-time Diary," March 23, 1941, in *Collected Essays*, 2:441.

11   George Orwell, "War-time Diary," July 28, 1942, in *Collected Essays*, 2:497; Orwell, "War-time Diary," October 11, 1942, in *Collected Essays*, 2:508; Orwell, "An Unpublished Letter to the Editor of *The Times*," in *Collected Essays*, 2:243–44.

12   Barry Lando, "Shocked by Trump? Churchill Wanted to 'Collar Them All,'" *CounterPunch*, November 24, 2015.

13   Alex Comfort, *No Such Liberty* (London: Chapman & Hall, 1941), 108–9.

14   George Orwell, "No, Not One."

15   Ibid.

16   George Orwell, "Politics vs. Literature: An Examination of *Gulliver's Travels*," *Polemic*, no. 5 (September 1946).

17   See Slavoj Zizek, "Stalinism," http://www.lacan.com/zizstalin.htm.

18   J. V. Stalin, "Concerning the International Situation," published in *Bolshevik*, no. 11 (September 20, 1924), reprinted in *Works*, vol. 6, January–November 1924 (Moscow: Foreign Languages Publishing, 1954), 293–314.

19   George Orwell, "London Letter." *Partisan Review*, March–April 1942.

20   Ibid.

21   "Vera Brittain: A Short Biography," Learn Peace, http://www.ppu.org.uk/learn/infodocs/people/pst_vera3.html.

22   "Comment on the Attitude of Gandhi and Other Congress Leaders," cited in George Orwell, *Orwell: The War Commentaries*, ed. W. J. West (New York: Pantheon, 1985), 19.

23   Alex Comfort, "On Interpreting the War," *Horizon*, May 1942.

24   Comfort, "1939 and 1984," 16.

25   John R. Doheny, letter to *Freedom*, no date, in Comfort Papers, University College London.

26   Alex Comfort, letter to *Tribune*, April 2, 1943.

27   Alex Comfort, "The Right Thing to Do," BBC talk, December 1948, published in *Freedom*, December 24, 1948, in Alex Comfort, *Writings against Power and Death*, ed. David Goodway (London: Freedom, 1994), 113.

28   Alex Comfort, "Art and Social Responsibility," in

Comfort, *Writings against Power and Death*, 56.

29   Cited in Overy, "Pacifism and the Blitz," 235.

30   George Orwell, "London Letter: The British Crisis," *Partisan Review*, July–August 1942, in *Collected Essays*, 2:249.

31   Cited in Lorna Waddington, *Hitler's Crusade: Bolshevism and the Myth of the International Jewish Conspiracy* (London: Tauris Academic Studies, 2007), 2.

32   Richard Griffiths, *Fellow Travellers of the Right: British Enthusiasts for Nazi Germany, 1933–39* (Oxford: Oxford University Press, 1983), 65–78.

33   Churchill, 1927, cited in George Orwell, "Who Are the War Criminals?," *Tribune*, November 26, 1943, in *Collected Essays*, 2:364.

34   Comfort, "1939 and 1984," 18.

35   See Orwell, "Who Are the War Criminals?," 363–69.

Chapter IV: A Disagreement in Verse

1   George Orwell, letter to Alex Comfort, July 15, 1942; and Comfort, letter to Orwell, July 16, 1942, in Davison, *Life in Letters*, 200–202.

2   Stephen Spender, "Modern Poets and Reviewers," *Horizon*, June 1942, cited in Arthur E. Salmon, *Alex Comfort* (Boston: Twayne, 1978), 106.

3   Meyers, *Wintry Conscience*, 216–17.

4   Woodcock, *Crystal Spirit*, 6.

5   George Orwell, letter to Dwight Macdonald, December 11, 1943, in Davison, *Life in Letters*, 223.

6   George Orwell, "Looking Back on the Spanish War," in *Collected Essays*, 2:300.

7   George Orwell, letter to Alex Comfort, July 11, 1943, in Davison, *Life in Letters*, 213.

8   George Orwell, letter to Alex Comfort, August 3, 1943, in *The Complete Works of George Orwell*, vol. 15: *Two Wasted Years*, ed. Peter Davison (London: Secker & Warburg, 1998), 180–81.

9   Dated May 28, 1943, in *The Complete Works of George Orwell*, vol. 13: *All Propaganda Is Lies*, ed. Peter Davison (London: Secker & Warburg, 1998), 341.

10   Alex Comfort, "Letter to an American Visitor, by Obadiah Hornbooke," *Tribune*, June 4, 1943.

11   George Orwell, letter to Alex Comfort, July 1943 [day unknown], in Davison, *Life in Letters*, 213.

12   George Orwell, letter to Alex Comfort, July 11, 1943, in Davison, *Life in Letters*, 213.

13   George Orwell, letter to Dwight Macdonald, December 11, 1943, in Davison, *Life in Letters*, 224; Orwell, cited in Kristian Williams, "'Two Wasted Years': Orwell at the BBC," *In These Times*, September 6, 2012.

14   Alex Comfort, interview with David Goodway, March 16, 1989.

15   Salmon, *Alex Comfort*, 64–67.

16   Reprinted in George Orwell, "The Meaning of Sabotage," pirated edition, no date.

17   George Orwell, "War-time Diary," June 30, 1940, in *Collected Essays*, 2:408.

18   George Orwell, letter to Alex Comfort, November 29, 1943, in *The Complete Works of George Orwell*, vol. 16: *I Have Tried to Tell the Truth*, ed. Peter Davison (London: Secker & Warburg, 1998), 9–10.

19   Alex Comfort, "The Little Apocalypse of Obadiah Hornbrook," *Tribune*, June 30, 1944.

20   George Orwell, "As I Please," *Tribune*, July 28, 1944. In what sense British imperialism could be worse than Nazism he did not explain.

21   George Orwell, letter to John Middleton Murry, July 21, 1944, in *The Collected Essays, Journalism and Letters of George Orwell*, vol. 3, *As I Please*, ed. Sonia Orwell and Ian Angus (London: Penguin, 1970), 237.

22   George Orwell, "As I Please," *Tribune*, September 1944.

23   Woodcock, *Crystal Spirit*, 252–53.

24   George Orwell, "London Letter to Partisan Review," *Partisan Review*, Summer 1946, in *The Collected Essays, Journalism and Letters of George Orwell*, vol. 4: *In Front of Your Nose*, ed. Sonia Orwell and Ian Angus (London: Penguin, 1970), 221.

25   Quoted in Jon Stallworthy, *Louis MacNeice: A Biography* (New York: W. W. Norton, 1995), 290.

Chapter V: Common Ground

1   See Ministry of Information report cited in *Orwell: The War Commentaries*, 20–22.

2   Orwell, *Collected Essays*, 3:438n; Alison Flood, "'It Needs More Public-Spirited Pigs': TS Eliot's Rejection of Orwell's Animal Farm," *Guardian*, May 26, 2016. Eliot disagreed with Orwell's

evident bias in *Animal Farm* as well, writing, "Your pigs are far more intelligent than the other animals, and therefore the best qualified to run the farm. . . . So what was needed was not more communism but more public-spirited pigs."

3   Letter to Arthur Koestler, September 20, 1947, cited in *Collected Essays*, 4:379.

4   In *Collected Essays*, 3:149–50.

5   George Orwell, "As I Please," *Tribune*, July 1944, in Comfort papers, University College London.

6   Stephen Spender, letter to Alex Comfort, January 25, 1944, in Comfort papers, University College London.

7   Comfort, "October, 1944."

8   W. P. Rilla, letter to Alex Comfort, October 6, 1944, in Comfort papers, University College London.

9   W. P. Rilla, letter to Alex Comfort, October 12, 1944, in Comfort papers, University College London.

10   W. P. Rilla, letters to Alex Comfort, October 16 and 18, 1944, in Comfort papers, University College London.

11   Robert Speaight, letter to Alex Comfort, October 23, 1944, in Comfort papers, University College London.

12   James Dempsey, "The Radical and the Aesthete: Randolph Bourne, Scofield Thayer, and *The Dial,*" *Revues modernistes* (Presses universitaires de Rennes, 2011), 151–59.

13   Quoted in John M. Curatola, "180 Degrees Out: The Change in U.S. Strategic Bombing Applications, 1935–1955" (PhD diss, University of Kansas, 2008), 83–84.

14   William L. Shirer, review of *Massacre by Bombing*, *New York Herald Tribune*, March 12, 1944.

15   George Orwell, "As I Please," *Tribune*, May 19, 1944.

16   George Orwell, "As I Please," *Tribune*, July 14, 1944.

17   Overy, "Constructing Space for Dissent," 611–12.

18   George Woodcock, *Letter to the Past: An Autobiography* (Toronto: Fitzhenry & Whiteside, 1982), 265.

19   Alex Comfort et al., "The Freedom Press Raid," letter to *New Statesman and Nation*, March 3, 1945.

20   Douglas Fetherling, *The Gentle Anarchist: The Life of George Woodcock* (Vancouver: Douglas & McIntyre, 1998), 41–42.

21   Woodcock, *Letter to the Past*, 268.

22   Ibid., 267.

23   Ibid., 283.

24   Ibid., 266.

25   George Orwell, "As I Please," *Tribune*, August 4, 1944, in *Collected Essays*, 3:233.

26   Christopher Hitchens, *Why Orwell Matters* (New York: Basic Books, 2002), 160.

27   Crick, *George Orwell: A Life*, 317.

28   Taylor, *Orwell: The Life*, 369.

29   David Goodway, *Anarchist Seeds beneath the Snow: Left-Libertarian Thought and British Writers from William Morris to Colin Ward* (Liverpool: Liverpool University Press, 2006), 135.

30   George Orwell, letter to Julian Symons, October 9, 1947, in *Collected Essays*, 4:380–81.

31   Goodway, *Anarchist Seeds*, 143–44.

32   Ibid., 125–29.

33   Emma Goldman, letter to Rose Pesotta, May 3, 1938, in Goldman Archive, XXVII A, cited in Goodway, *Anarchist Seeds*, 135.

34   Letter to Herbert Read, March 5, 1939, in *Collected Essays*, 1:424.

35   Alex Comfort, "Criminal Lunacy Exposed," *War Commentary*, August 25, 1945.

36   George Orwell, "You and the Atomic Bomb," *Tribune*, October 19, 1945.

37   Alex Comfort, "Us and the Atom Bomb," *Tribune*, October 26, 1945.

38   Alex Comfort, *Peace and Disobedience*, pamphlet (London: *Peace News*, 1946).

39   Alex Comfort, "An Anarchist View: The Political Relevance of Pacifism," *Peace News*, December 7, 1945.

40   George Orwell, "London Letter," *Partisan Review*, Winter 1944, in *Collected Essays*, 3:339.

Chapter VI: The Sociopathic State

1   Comfort, "1939 and 1984," 17.

2   Gwyneth Roberts, introduction to *Nineteen Eighty-Four* by George Orwell (London: Longman Group, 1983).

3   Comfort, "1939 and 1984," 22.

4   Taylor, *Orwell: The Life*, 389.

5   Julian Symons, introduction to *Nineteen Eighty-Four*, Everyman's Library (New York: Alfred A. Knopf, 1992), xx.

6   Alex Comfort, *Art and Social Responsibility: Lectures on the Ideology of Romanticism* (London: Falcon, 1946).

7   Flewers, "I Know How, but I Don't Know Why," 14.

8   Letter to Dwight Macdonald, December 5, 1946, in Davison, *Life in Letters*, 334.

9   Alex Comfort, *Authority and Delinquency in the Modern State: A Criminological Approach to the Problem of Power* (London: Sphere Books, 1970). This and the quotes that follow are from the slightly revised 1970 edition.

10   Ibid., 11.

11   Mikhail Bakunin, "Power Corrupts the Best" (1867), *Anarchy Archives*, http://dwardmac.pitzer.edu/Anarchist_Archives/bakunin/bakuninpower.html.

12   Comfort, *Authority and Delinquency*, 21.

13   Ibid., 42.

14   Ibid.

15   Ibid., 99.

16   Quoted in *Women's Own*, October 31, 1987.

17   Comfort, *Authority and Delinquency*, 103–4.

18   Sebald, "Air War and Literature," 19.

19   Comfort, "1939 and 1984," 21.

20   Comfort, *Authority and Delinquency*, 116–19.

21   Ibid., 118.

22   Cited in *The Complete Works of George Orwell*, vol. 18: *Smothered under Journalism*, ed. Peter Davison (London: Secker & Warburg, 1998), 507.

23   Quoted in Goodway, *Anarchist Seeds*, 251.

24   Sebastian de Grazia, *Machiavelli in Hell* (New York: Vintage Books, 1994), 273, 268–69.

25   Herbert Read, *Education for Peace* (New York: Charles Scribner's Sons, 1949), 38.

26   Herbert Read, *Education through Art*, 2nd ed. (London: Faber & Faber, 1945), 5.

27   Cited in Goodway, *Anarchist Seeds*, 252.

28   Comfort, *Art and Social Responsibility*, 29.

29   Quoted in Peter Davison and D. J. Taylor, "Like Autumn in a Garden: New Light on the Friendship between George Orwell and Malcolm Muggeridge," *Times Literary Supplement*, May 30, 2003.

30   Murray Bookchin, "Ecology and Revolutionary Thought," *Anarchy*, 1965, http://dwardmac.pitzer.edu/Anarchist_Archives/bookchin/ecologyandrev.html.

31   See Alex Comfort, *Sex in Society* (London: Gerald Duckworth, 1963).

Chapter VII: The "Snitch List"

1   Interview with Nicholas Comfort, November 21, 2016.

2   Quoted in Meyers, *Wintry Conscience*, 196.

3   In *Collected Essays*, 4:355.

4   George Orwell, "Notes on Nationalism," *Polemic*, October 1945.

5   George Orwell, letter to Arthur Koestler, March 21, 1947, in Davison, *Life in Letters*, 200.

6   George Orwell, "Politics vs. Literature," *Polemic*, September 1946, in *Collected Essays*, 4:252.

7   Orwell finished the novel at the end of 1948. Julian Symons, introduction to *Nineteen Eighty-Four*, xix.

8   Peter Davison, note, in Davison, *Lost Orwell*, 140–41.

9   Included in Davison, *Lost Orwell*, 142.

10   Interview with Nicholas Comfort, November 21, 2016.

11   George Orwell to Richard Rees, April 6, 1949, cited in Hitchens, *Why Orwell Matters*, 162.

12   Unity Theatre, unknown author, letter to Alex Comfort, August 20, 1941, in Comfort papers, University College London.

13   Hitchens, *Why Orwell Matters*, 157.

14   Quoted in Timothy Garton Ash, "Orwell's List," *New York Review of Books*, September 25, 2003.

15   Flewers, "I Know How, but I Don't Know Why," 29.

16   Nicholas Moore, letter to Arthur Salmon, September 29, 1980.

17   Alexander Cockburn, "St. George's List," *Nation*, December 7, 1998.

18   Ros Wynne-Jones, "Orwell's Little List Leaves the Left Gasping for More," *Independent*, July 14, 1996.

19   Fiachra Gibbons, "Blacklisted Writer Says Illness Clouded Orwell's Judgment," *Guardian*, June 24, 2003.

20   Tom Utley, "Orwell Is Revealed in Role of State Informer," *Daily Telegraph*, July 12, 1996.

21   Hitchens, *Why Orwell Matters*, 169.

22   Garton Ash, "Orwell's List."

23   Frances Stoner Saunders, *The Cultural Cold War: The CIA and the World of Arts and Letters (New York: The New Press, 1999)*, 59.

24   Ibid., 299; Saunders's italics.

25   Garton Ash, "Orwell's List."

26   Comfort, "1939 and 1984," 20.

Chapter VIII:

1   Comfort, "1939 and 1984," 16.

2   Quoted in Meyers, *Wintry Conscience*, 196.

3   George Orwell, *Homage to Catalonia* (New York: Harcourt Brace Jovanovich, 1952), 4.

4   George Orwell to Geoffrey Gorer, quoted in Meyers, *Wintry Conscience*, 195.

5   George Orwell, "War-time Diary," April 27, 1942, in *Collected Essays*, 2:478.

6   Alex Comfort, *The Pattern of the Future: Four Broadcast Talks* (London: Routledge & Kegan Paul, 1949), 16.

7   Kristian Williams, *Between the Bullet and the Lie: Essays on Orwell* (Oakland: AK Press, 2017), 78.

8   Rufus Burrow Jr., *Martin Luther King, Jr., and the Theology of Resistance* (Jefferson, NC: McFarland, 2014), 41.

9   Ibid., 41.

10   Clayborne Carson, introduction to *The Papers of Martin Luther King, Jr: Birth of a New Age, December 1955*, ed. Clayborne Carson (Berkeley: University of California Press, 1997), 17.

11   Alex Comfort, "Art and Social Responsibility" (London: Falcon, 1946), in *Against Power and Death*, 73, 76–77.

12   Quoted in Lovia Gyarke, "James Baldwin and the Struggle to Bear Witness," *New Republic*, February 3, 2017.

13   George Orwell, "Revenge Is Sour," in *Collected Essays*, 4:3–4.

14   George Orwell, "As I Please," *Tribune*, September 8, 1944.

Chapter IX: Conclusion

1   Orwell, "London Letter."

2   Alex Comfort, "What Can We Do to Stop Them?," *Freedom*, April 14, 1951.

3   Author, interviews with Zhores A. Medvedev, February 18 and 23, 2010.

4   Alex Comfort, "Letter after America," *Freedom*, October 1986.

5   Alex Comfort, "As I Please," *Tribune*, October 17, 1947.

6   George Orwell, "In Defence of Comrade Zilliacus," in *Collected Essays*, 4:451–53.

7   Mary McCarthy, "The Writing on the Wall," *New York Review of Books*, January 30, 1969.

8   Norman Podhoretz, "If Orwell Were Alive Today," *Harper's*, January 1983.

9   Woodcock, *Crystal Spirit*, 283.

10   Pierre-Joseph Proudhon, *Correspondance*, vol. 4 (Paris: éditions Lacroix, 1875), 376, cited in Edouard Jourdain, "Justice and Utopia: Reading Ricouer and Proudhon Together," trans. Jesse Cohn, *Philosophy Today* 58, no. 14 (2014): 527–55.

11   Nicolas Walter, "Orwell and the Pacifists," *Peace News*, November 1, 1968, in Rodden, *Politics of Literary Reputation*.

12   Mary McCarthy, "The Writing on the Wall."

13   George Orwell, afterword to German translation of "The Intellectual Revolt," April 1946, in *Complete Works*, 18:70–71.

14   George Orwell, "Pacifism and Progress," *Manchester Evening News*, February 14, 1946, in *Complete Works*, 18:67.

15   Ibid., 68–69.

16   Ibid., 69.

17   Woodcock, *The Crystal Spirit*, 312.

18   Henry Probert, *Bomber Harris: His Life and Times* (London: Greenhill Books, 2006), 346–51; Sir Arthur Harris, *Bomber Offensive* (London: Greenhill Books, 2005), 242.

19   Blaine Harden, "The U.S. War Crime North Korea Won't Forget," *Washington Post*, March 24, 2015; Daniel Read, "History and Hypocrisy: Why the Korean War Matters in the Age of Trump," *CounterPunch*, May 8, 2017; Christine Hog, radio interview, *Democracy Now!*, April 17, 2017.

20   "Unacknowledged Deaths: Civilian Casualties in NATO's Air Campaign in Libya," Human Rights Watch report, May 13, 2012, https://www.hrw.org/report/2012/05/13/unacknowledged-deaths/civilian-casualties-natos-air-campaign-libya.

21   "Hannover Evacuates 50,000 over World War Two Bombs," *BBC News*, May 7, 2017.

22   Thomas Gibbons-Neff, "The Pentagon Said It Wouldn't Use Depleted Uranium Rounds against ISIS. Months Later, It Did—Thousands of Times," *Washington Post*, February 16, 2017.

23   "Vast Undercount of Mosul Dead: 9,000 Civilians Paid in Blood," *New York Times*, December 20, 2017.

INDEX

Page numbers in *italic* refer to illustrations. "Passim" (literally "scattered") indicates intermittent discussion of a topic over a cluster of pages.

A

Acton, John Emerich Edward Dalberg Acton, Baron, 100
actors and actresses, 11, 32–33, 118
Adelphi, 11, 40, 47, 55, 70
African American church, 128
Albarn, David, 38
Albarn, Edmund, 38
Aldermaston marches, 138–39
America First movement, 15, 45
Amritsar massacre, 52
Anand, Mulk Raj, *57*
anarchism, 109, 113, 127; Orwell views, 13, 17, 86, 115, 142–45 passim
Animal Farm (Orwell), 12, 73–74, 85, 86, 98, 103–8 passim, 142; copy given to Camus, 145; Smollett and, 118n; translated editions, 117
antinuclear movement. *See* nuclear disarmament movement
antiwar movement, 16, 23–24, 25, 32, 37, 38, 50, 90; Special Branch raid of, 82–85. *See also* Peace Pledge Union (PPU); *War Commentary*
"area bombing." *See* bombing of civilians
Art and Social Responsibility (Comfort), 97, 119, 129–30
artists and writers, responsibility of, 13, 16, 50, 76, 126, 129–30
"An Atoll of the Mind" (Comfort), 48, 56
atomic bomb, 2, 88–90 passim, 91, 99
Auden, W. H., 20, 21, 61
Australia, 41
Authority and Delinquency in the Modern State: A Criminological Approach to the Problem of Power (Comfort), 4, 12–13, 98–103 passim, *99*, 112, 119
Authorization for Use of Military Force (United States), 100–101, 151

B

Bakunin, Mikhail, 100
Baldwin, James, 128, 130
Bayliss, John, 20, 57–58
BBC, 7, 19, 20, 47, 56–57, *57*, 112, 122; Comfort, 60, 61, 68, 76–78, 82, 120, 127; MacNeice, 61; Michael Redgrave ban, 32–33; *Nineteen Eighty-Four* basis on, 94; Orwell resignation, 65, 68; Orwell "snitch list" and, 12; party line on India, 48; party line on USSR, 73; Read, *57*, 119; on unexploded World War II ordnance, 150
Bedford, Hastings Russell, Duke of, 44, 46
Bell, George, 37
Berneri, Marie Louise, 45, 83–88 passim, *87*, 94n
Bevan, Aneurin, 62, 138
Big Brother (Orwell), 94, 96–97, 103–4, 113, 122, 127–28, 132, 143
biological weapons, 31, 147
Blair, Richard, 112
Blunden, Edmund, 57, *57*
Bomber Command (RAF). *See* Royal Air Force (RAF): Bomber Command

AK Press is small, in terms of staff and resources, but we also manage to be one of the world's most productive anarchist publishing houses. We publish close to twenty books every year, and distribute thousands of other titles published by like-minded independent presses and projects from around the globe. We're entirely worker-run and democratically managed. We operate without a corporate structure—no boss, no managers, no bullshit.

The Friends of AK program is a way you can directly contribute to the continued existence of AK Press, and ensure that we're able to keep publishing books like this one! Friends pay $25 a month directly into our publishing account ($30 for Canada, $35 for international), and receive a copy of every book AK Press publishes for the duration of their membership! Friends also receive a discount on anything they order from our website or buy at a table: 50% on AK titles, and 20% on everything else. We have a Friends of AK ebook program as well: $15 a month gets you an electronic copy of every book we publish for the duration of your membership. You can even sponsor a very discounted membership for someone in prison.

Email FRIENDSOFAK@AKPRESS.ORG for more info, or visit the Friends of AK Press website: HTTPS://WWW.AKPRESS.ORG/FRIENDS.HTML.

There are always great book projects in the works—so sign up now to become a Friend of AK Press, and let the presses roll!